Dezeen Book of Ideas

Edited by Marcus Fairs

Published by Spotlight Press

First published in 2011
by Spotlight Press Ltd
www.dezeenbookofideas.com

Editor: Marcus Fairs
Assistant editor:
Alexandra Constantinides
Sub-editor: Esme Fieldhouse
Writers:
Alexandra Constantinides,
Rose Etherington, Marcus Fairs,
Esme Fieldhouse, Amy Frearson
Design: Micha Weidmann Studio
Publisher: Max Fraser

British Library Cataloguing-in-
Publication data. A catalogue
record for this book is available
from the British Library.

Printed in the UK
by Butler Tanner & Dennis.

Trade orders: Central Books,
orders@centralbooks.com
www.centralbooks.com

ISBN 978-0-9563098-2-2

Contents

Introduction
by Marcus Fairs

Ideas are easy; ideas are free.
Turning ideas into reality is the hard bit.

This book contains 116 ideas that
have made the biggest impression on
us at www.dezeen.com, and which
have received the biggest reaction from
our million-strong global readership.

Some of the ideas are profound, some
of them are beautiful, and some are just
plain absurd. Not all of them have made
the difficult journey from computer
rendering to physical reality – a few of
them never will.

But collectively the ideas in this book
give a fascinating overview of the way
today's leading architects and designers
are thinking, as well as offering a taster
of the incredible diversity of projects
we have published on Dezeen in the five
years since we launched.

There are 116 projects in this book: 40 architecture, 22 interiors and 54 design.

The projects are all mixed up together rather than being arranged according to type, to create the same unexpected juxtapositions that occur on our website.

Refer to the Links section starting on page 196 for details of where to find more information about each idea.

Every image in this book is square, in line with Dezeen's policy of only publishing square images on its home page (because they look nice).

Look out for the top ten stories, which are the most popular published on Dezeen at the time of going to press. They can be found on pages 46, 50, 52, 66, 72, 78, 112, 160, 176 and 188.

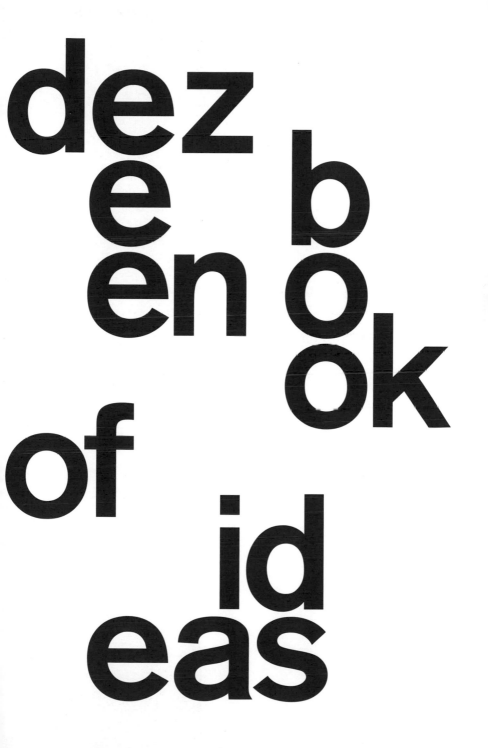

dezeen book of ideas

Plumen 001
Hulger

The light bulb has long served as a metaphor for human ingenuity. But with the phasing out of traditional incandescent light bulbs, this low-energy designer bulb is a new symbol of creative brilliance.

Using 80 per cent less energy than a traditional bulb, the Plumen 001 is described by its manufacturers as 'the world's first designer low-energy light bulb' and is intended to reinvent the ugly compact fluorescent lamp (CFL) as an object of beauty.

Instead of the ungainly prongs or whirls of the standard CFL, Plumen 001 features two graceful loops that give the product a different profile according to the position it is viewed from. In a nod to its predecessor, it takes on the shape of a traditional bulb from certain angles (pictured).

Unlike most CFLs, which lighting designers try to hide, the Plumen 001 is designed to be seen, either displayed naked at the end of a flex or mounted conspicuously in a lighting fixture. »

» Hulger, the British brand behind the product, has encouraged customers to upload photos to its Flickr account and the results show the bulbs inserted into everything from 20th century design classics to ornate Venetian-style lamps.

The name Plumen refers to both the showy plumage of birds and lumen, the term used to measure the power of lighting output.

Launched in 2010, the Plumen 001 was designed by Hulger in collaboration with British designer Sam Wilkinson. In 2011 it won the coveted Brit Insurance Design of the Year award, announced at the London Design Museum.

It is the first in what will eventually become a family of low-energy lighting products.

Sliding House
dRMM

The roof and walls of this family home move on rails, transforming the hall into an open-air courtyard and the living quarters into a double-height conservatory.

The 28-metre long mobile structure fits like a sleeve over the main house, the guest annex and the paved yard that separates the two.

Powered by electric motors and remote control, an ever-changing series of spaces and light conditions is created as the structure moves.

Tough planning restrictions in this rural corner of England meant that London-based architects dRMM had to design the house in a manner sympathetic with the local farm vernacular. Hence all of the structures are versions of the archetypal Suffolk barn. The house, annex and garage – which is the only

structure to sit off the linear axis –
are clad in red and black stained
timber. The 20-tonne, steel-framed
rolling element is weather-boarded
in untreated larch, with a red rubber
membrane on the inside.

The house was completed at the
beginning of 2009. A proposal to
extend the run of the mobile
structure over a swimming pool
has yet to be realised. For another
farm-inspired house in Suffolk,
see the Balancing Barn on page 28.

Corpus 2.0
Marcia Nolte

Instead of products being designed
around the human body, what if
the body adapted itself around
products? This series of digitally
manipulated portraits imagines
how the human form could evolve
in response to technology, fashion
and lifestyle habits.

The project, called Corpus 2.0,
was developed by Dutch designer
Marcia Nolte for her 2008 graduation show at Design Academy
Eindhoven in the Netherlands.
The series of images shows men and
women who each have one mutated
body part. It generated a wide range
of responses in Dezeen's comments
section, ranging from fascination
to revulsion.

Smokinghole imagines that
smokers have evolved a hole in
their lips to better accommodate
a cigarette (pictured), while
Headphone-ear envisages the
human ear evolving a vertical slot so
that in-ear headphones fit perfectly,
stopping them from falling out and
preventing sound from escaping. »

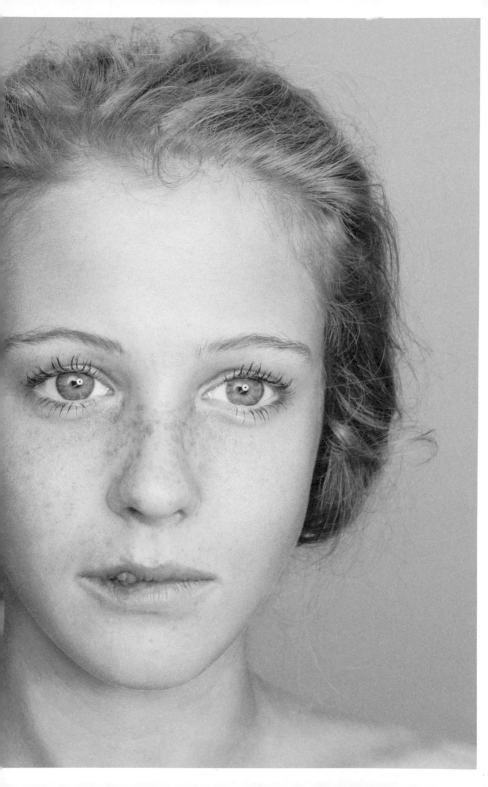

» Other images in the series include Noseslope – a horizontal ridge on the bridge of the nose that holds glasses in place, removing the need for frames that are supported by the ears (pictured) – and Shoulderholder, which is a bulbous, extended shoulder that more easily holds a phone against the ear, meaning you can talk to a friend and still have both hands free for other tasks.

High-heel Foot shows a woman whose feet have permanently adapted to wearing high-heeled shoes. The most plausible image in the series is Touch-it Thumb, in which the thumb has become disproportionately enlarged due to extensive use sending text messages and playing computer games.

Selexyz
Dominicanen
Merkx + Girod
Architecten

There are a lot of empty churches in the Netherlands, but this one in Maastricht has found an unexpected new lease of life as a bookshop.

A deconsecrated 13th-century Dominican church in the city centre had previously been used as a bicycle storage depot and a warehouse, until it was converted into a new branch of Dutch bookstore chain Selexyz in 2007.

With a floor area of just 750 square metres, architects Merkx + Girod had no option but to exploit the height of the nave and so inserted a three-storey, steel structure bookshelf along one side of the church interior.

This building-within-a-building solution keeps the floor of the church uncluttered, allowing the historic building to be appreciated, while providing 1,200 square metres of retail floor space.

The church was restored and given a new lighting scheme as part of the project. The crypt is used for services and storage.

With the hush of prayer now replaced by the hush of book browsing, Selexyz Dominicanen has been widely acclaimed as a model for the reuse of unwanted buildings. The architecture critic at UK newspaper The Guardian, Jonathan Glancey, reviewed the project following its publication on Dezeen and called it 'one of the finest bookshops in the world'.

Receipt redesign
BERG

Boring restaurant receipts become educational and entertaining in this rethink by London design consultancy BERG.

Rather than simply listing the amount paid, the thermal printout provides a mixture of nutritional information and trivia about the food purchased, as well as marketing messages and tick boxes to allow customers to provide feedback.

BERG was asked to reinvent the receipt for a feature in Icon magazine, which each month invites designers to redesign a familiar object. The receipt appeared in the magazine's July 2011 issue.

The new-look proof of purchase takes dry numerical data recorded by the cash register and presents it as a mixture of auto-generated text and info-graphics. Graphs show the popularity of items at different times of the day while fact boxes tell the diner the total number of calories and the percentage of their recommended daily allowance they have consumed.

With information about forthcoming promotions and discount offers, the receipt doubles as a publicity-generating flyer for the establishment, as the customer is likely to retain it for future use and show it to friends.

BERG says the concept is viable, as modern cash registers already possess the computing power and printing technology to generate more informative sales slips.

Rubber House
Zeinstra
van Gelderen

Cast entirely in amber-coloured urethane resin, the Rubber House is notable for its strange material properties rather than its form.

Access to the stretchy pavilion is via a vertical slice in the wall. Inside is an egg-shaped void large enough for one person. A moulded seat faces towards a window that cannot be seen through – a parody of the traditionally contemplative 'room with a view'.

Designed by Dutch architects Zeinstra van Gelderen, the womb-like qualities prompted one Dezeen reader to comment that it appears to be giving birth to people exiting the structure.

The folly was created in 2010 and exhibited at a series of festivals and conferences in Germany.

Inntel Hotel
WAM Architecten

Instead of applying a generic contemporary aesthetic to this landmark hotel, Dutch architects WAM Architecten collected examples of the regional vernacular and piled them on top of each other.

Replicas of almost seventy houses make up the façade of the 12-storey Inntel Hotel in Zaandam, capital of the Dutch region of Zaanstad. It is a cut-and-paste conglomeration of traditional timber dwellings with gable ends, ranging from modest workers' cottages to lawyers' mansions.

Each house is one of four shades of green seen on buildings locally, with one exception: among them is an approximation of the 'Blue House', a famous canal-side property in the city painted by Claude Monet in 1871.

The 160-room hotel was completed in 2010 and sits in a regenerated district consisting of traditionally inspired streets and houses.

The T-Shirt Issue
Mashallah Design
& Linda Kostowski

Bespoke tailoring is taken to a new level with these custom-made T-shirts that incorporate forms based on the personal memories of the wearer.

To generate the highly personalised garments, Mashallah Design and Linda Kostowski scanned people's bodies in three dimensions and interviewed them to unearth meaningful images from their experiences or dreams.

The data and the imagery was then digitally combined to create a series of polygons that, when laser cut from fabric and stitched together, form a perfectly fitting T-shirt with a unique sculptural addition.

The Wolf T-Shirt (pictured) features a fabric wolf head attached to the shoulder. This was created for someone who, as a boy, heard the story of a child being brought up by wolves and subsequently imagined he had a wolf-friend of his own.

The garments are made from thick jersey material and designed in 3D modelling software more commonly used to design industrial products. To generate the dozens of flat polygons required to assemble the items, the Berlin-based designers used the software's 'unfold' function, which turns a three-dimensional object into a 2D pattern that can be used to create a paper model.

The T-Shirt Issue was presented at the CREATE Berlin exhibition in London in 2008, during the London Design Festival.

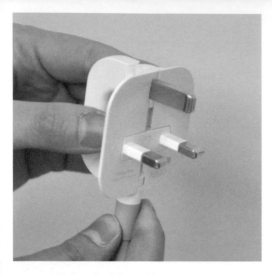

Folding Plug
Min-Kyu Choi

When the standard UK electrical plug – the world's biggest – was introduced in the 1940s, consumer electronic devices such as televisions and radios were bulky and immovable.

Yet while gadgets today are increasingly tiny and designed for use on the move, the plug has not evolved at all – it is, in fact, often bigger than the device it recharges.

Korean designer Min-Kyu Choi designed his Folding Plug in 2009, while a student at the Royal College of Art in London, to make life easier for people who travel regularly.

When not in use, the plastic case folds in half while the brass pins that carry the positive and neutral charge rotate to align with the earth pin, flattening the plug to a thickness of just 10 millimetres. Another design feature is that the pins have rounded, not faceted, ends to prevent them scratching other items during transit.

The young graduate also made sure that his plug follows British Standard 1363, met by the conventional three-pin UK plug.

The Folding Plug won the Brit Insurance Design of the Year Award in 2010, with judges praising Choi for his efforts to improve a banal everyday object, which is often overlooked by designers.

Cloud City
Studio Lindfors

Residents could seek temporary refuge in an airborne city of balloons if a devastating coastal storm were to inundate New York, according to this proposal by New York-based Studio Lindfors.

Cloud City was their entry for the What if New York City... competition, launched in 2007 to design temporary post-disaster housing.

The helium-filled balloons would be stored in warehouses and rapidly deployed when required. Each would contain a 28 square metre living space encompassing a kitchen and bathroom core.

The hovering homes would keep the ground free of obstructions for reconstruction work and enable survivors to remain close to their community, playing an active part in the rebuilding process.

Balancing Barn
MVRDV

The banal agricultural architecture of Suffolk, England, provided the inspiration for this holiday home. Dutch architects MVRDV took the simple form and metal cladding of the farm vernacular but added a twist: the house balances atop a steep bank and dramatically cantilevers over the drop like an inhabitable diving board.

Measuring 30 metres in length, half of the building's volume is suspended in the air. At the highest point, there is a swing hanging underneath. Internally, the house is arranged as a linear progression, with the kitchen-diner first, bedrooms arranged along a corridor in the middle, and the lounge at the furthest end. A large glass panel on the floor of the lounge reminds visitors that they are airborne.

The house was completed in autumn 2010 and formed the first in a series of holiday homes in the English countryside designed by leading contemporary architects such as NORD and Peter Zumthor. They have been commissioned by Living Architecture, a project initiated by writer Alain de Botton to make the experience of good modern architecture and design more accessible.

A Flip Flop Story
Diederik Schneemann

Every year ten tonnes of flip-flops, mainly originating from Asia, wash up onto the beaches of eastern Africa. Dutch designer Diederik Schneemann has turned this seafaring footwear, which according to him is 'trodden on, travelled with, badgered and scarred but still moving on,' into a series of multi-coloured domestic objects.

The flip-flops are collected from the shore and taken to a factory in Nairobi where they are recycled into products including a table ornament on wheels (pictured), a vase with a built-in drawer and a table lamp with an integrated power socket.

The project, called A Flip Flop Story, is in collaboration with the UniquEco Foundation, a local organisation that employs people to salvage unwanted materials and turn them into craft objects.

The PVC foam soles are sanded to remove the dirt and reveal the original bright colours, 80 per cent of which are either blue or red. The material is then cut into squares and glued in layers to build a solid block from which objects can be carved.

The vibrant colours of the flip-flops inspired Schneemann to design toy-like products that reference the cranes, trucks, tanks and planes, which fascinated him as a child. Hence most of the flip-flop products feature wheels.

The range was launched at the 2011 Object Rotterdam design show.

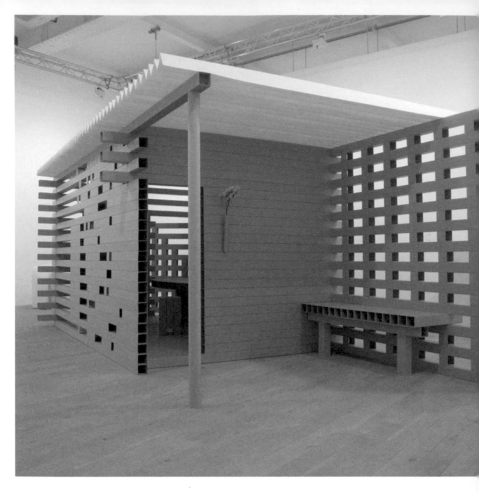

Paper Tea House
Shigeru Ban

Traditional Japanese teahouses often feature paper screens but Shigeru Ban has used paper and cardboard for almost every part of this contemporary version.

The five-metre long Paper Tea House, designed to sit within a larger building, has walls that are constructed from square paper tubes and a roof of folded paper. The only non-paper elements are steel rods hidden inside the walls that tie the structure together.

The specially designed furniture is also made of cardboard. A series of stools, shelving and a bench are made of the same square tubes as the walls while a table is made from honeycomb cardboard.

The Japanese architect has forged a career out of paper and cardboard architecture, starting in

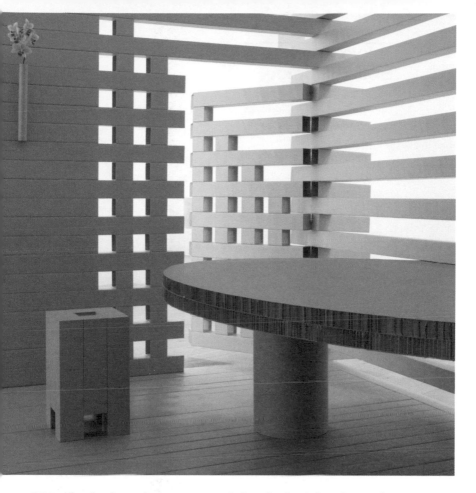

1989 with a circular outdoor pavilion made from giant paper tubes that are normally used as moulds for concrete columns.

Since then Ban has tested the structural limits of paper tubes on a range of projects including bridges, exhibition halls and churches.

As a building material, paper tubes are lightweight and relatively easy to transport. Ban has explored using the material for humanitarian purposes, by designing housing solutions for the victims of war and natural disasters. In 2011 he designed a cardboard tube system for dividing large buildings such as sports halls into temporary accommodation to house people displaced by the Japanese earthquake and tsunami.

Dezeen published Paper Tea House in 2008, the day before it was due to be sold at London auctioneer Phillips de Pury. It sold for £31,700, higher than the pre-sale estimate.

Tokyo Apartment
Sou Fujimoto

Tokyo city centre features streets of
low-rise houses crammed between
high-rise apartment blocks. This
development by Japanese architect
Sou Fujimoto is a curious hybrid of
the two.

Located on a street corner in a
central residential neighbourhood,
Tokyo Apartment features
archetypal house-shaped units
stacked askew to create a miniature
tower of tiny homes.

The three-storey block contains
four dwellings altogether – one
belonging to the owner and three for
rent. Each has its own front door
and features two or three separate
rooms linked by internal ladders.

The upper units are reached by
twisting staircases that traverse the
roofs of lower blocks. Resembling
the wooden stairs used in mountainous parts of Japan, these give
residents the impression that they
live atop their own private hill,
rather than in a teeming metropolis.

Tokyo Apartment is both a smart
visual joke and a clever attempt to
give apartment dwellers the sense of
ownership and security that comes
with a traditional-style home. »

» The project was completed in 2010, around the same time that Swiss architects Herzog & de Meuron completed VitraHaus, a furniture showroom for design brand Vitra at its headquarters in Weil am Rhein, Germany. Vitra-Haus also features a dramatic stack of house-shaped units, suggesting that leading contemporary architects are increasingly intrigued by the psychological importance of the basic house form.

The photographs of Tokyo Apartment were taken by British architectural photographer Edmund Sumner, who travels to Japan regularly and has provided images for several architectural projects in this book.

Honeycomb Vase
Studio Libertiny

Forty thousand bees spent a week making this vase. They used thousands of blobs of beeswax to build up the honeycomb structure in a process akin to rapid prototyping – albeit much slower and less predictable.

Slovakian designer Tomáš Gabzdil Libertiny of Studio Libertiny describes the production method as 'slow prototyping'. He initiated the process by making a template using beeswax sheets, embossed with a tessellated hexagon pattern, and placing it inside a beehive. The worker bees then set about turning it into honeycomb.

The first Honeycomb Vase was exhibited during the Milan furniture fair in April 2007. Libertiny's bees then went on to produce a series of limited edition vases called Made by Bees (pictured), each of which vary in colour, form and smell, depending on the location of the hive, the species of flowers in season and the amount of time given to the honey bees to do their work.

The vases have acquired unintended cultural poignancy due to the American media reporting on the unexplained collapse of bee colonies across the country in the month they were first exhibited.

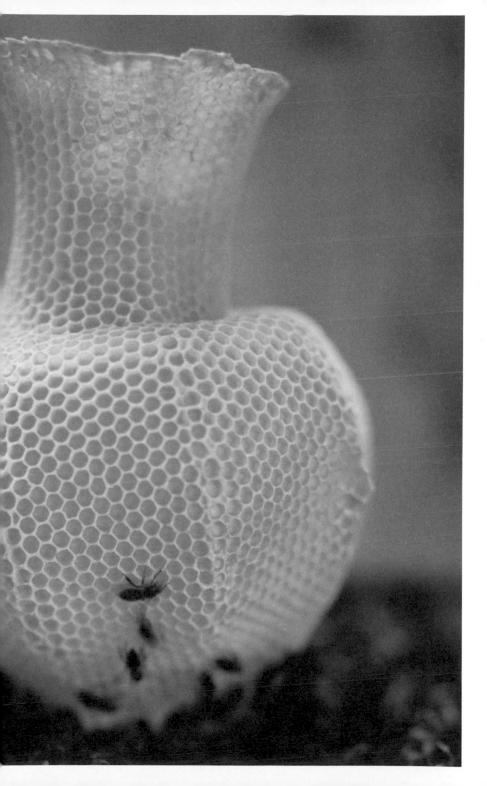

GINA Light Visionary Model BMW

Cars, like aeroplanes and ships, are usually constructed of rigid materials that retain their shape at all times. Yet the optimum shape of a vehicle changes according to the conditions; a streamlined profile is better at high speed, while a compact form is preferable when stationary, so the car takes up less parking space.

The GINA Light Visionary Model is a concept car by BMW featuring a high-tech fabric skin stretched over a skeletal metal frame, which is articulated to allow movement. As it moves, the fabric adapts to the new form, like the skin of a living creature: the hidden headlights open and blink like eyes, the bonnet gapes for maintenance like a mouth, and the doors unfold like wings (top image). The frame also shifts to adopt a stealthier profile when travelling at speed (bottom image).

A fabric body requires far fewer panels than a traditional car – just four in this case – and would theoretically be cheaper to manufacture than today's pressed metal and moulded plastic components. It would also offer the possibility of giving customers uniquely shaped cars, instead of the standard models on offer today.

GINA, which stands for Geometry and Functions In 'N' Adaptations, was unveiled in June 2008.

The Virgin Collection OAT

Instead of throwing these shoes away when they wear out, you can plant them. Seeds embedded in the tongue sprout into flowers as the biodegradable shoes decompose.

Dutch designers OAT launched the range, called The Virgin Collection, at Amsterdam International Fashion Week in January 2011, where they won The Green Fashion Competition. Their runway show was called Saved from the Garden of Eden and featured the trainers planted in white wheelbarrows, pushed by models dressed as Adam and Eve.

The collection comprises four designs, available in a combination of white and beige canvas, which range from high-tops to a more classic tennis sneaker-style. OAT themselves describe the footwear as 'vintage-killers': rather than ending up in second-hand shops and becoming classics, their final resting place is intended to be the garden.

Their intentional transience contrasts with the long-term waste problem created by plastic footwear, which ends up in landfill or, in the case of Asian flip-flops, as ocean flotsam on African beaches (see A Flip Flop Story on page 30).

Serpentine Gallery Pavilion Various

Each year, a leading international architect is asked to design a summer pavilion for the lawns outside the Serpentine Gallery in London's Kensington Gardens.

Serving as a temporary tourist attraction, event space, café and venue-for-hire, the pavilion is a highly successful fundraiser and marketing tool for the gallery itself, hosting the Serpentine's star-studded annual summer party.

It also gives the public a rare opportunity to experience avant-garde architecture and as a result has done much to stimulate popular debate about the discipline.

For the architects, who – like most people involved – are not paid for their services, the pavilion is a high-profile commission that allows

them to experiment with new ideas and forms. They must also work at a breakneck pace, which sees an initial idea turned into reality in a matter of months, rather than years.

The brief has barely changed since Zaha Hadid was invited to design the first pavilion in 2000; the temporary structure invariably sits on the same patch, there is a maximum time period of six months from invitation to completion, and it must last three months. It is always »

» programmatically simple: a space for hosting events and perhaps somewhere to buy a drink too.

Hadid's inaugural pavilion was a steel-framed marquee with a zigzag roof and 2011's was a walled garden by Peter Zumthor; the intervening years have featured aluminium origami (Daniel Libeskind in 2001), a red shed (Jean Nouvel in 2010), and a giant helium balloon (Rem Koolhaas in 2006).

The only break came in 2004 when MVRDV's turfed mountain, which was to be constructed over the gallery, proved too ambitious.

Pictured here are pavilions by Jean Nouvel, 2010, and SANAA, 2009 (previous page); Peter Zumthor, 2011, and Frank Gehry, 2008 (this page).

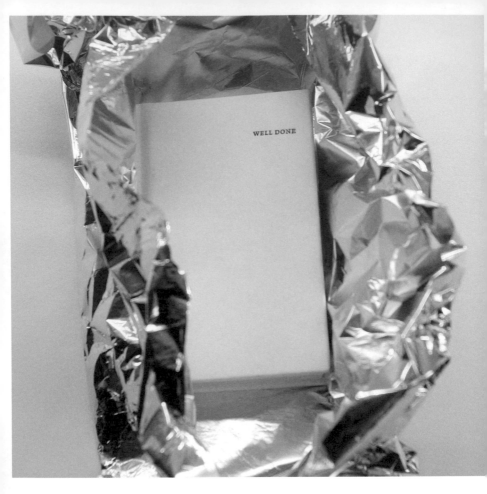

Top ten #1

Well Done
Bruketa & Žinić

In 2007, Croatian food brand Podravka produced an annual report that had to be put in the oven and baked before you could read it.

Called Well Done, it was developed by Zagreb-based creative agency Bruketa & Žinić and featured blank pages printed with thermo-reactive ink.

The oven-ready booklet came hidden inside a more traditional corporate report containing financial data.

Invisible text and images printed in the booklet were only revealed if you wrapped it in aluminium foil and baked it at 100 degrees Celsius for precisely 25 minutes. Cooking it for longer than this would cause the booklet to burn.

People who followed instructions carefully were rewarded with a

range of recipes featuring Podravka
ingredients that appeared on
formerly blank pages, plus images
of food that manifested themselves
on illustrations of plates that were
empty before baking.

Well Done is the most popular
story ever published on Dezeen, and
has been seen by over a quarter of a
million people to date.

Mojito Shoes
Julian Hakes

Conventional shoes are assembled from many separate parts and are engineered to support the whole foot. These shoes by architect Julian Hakes are made of a single component and leave the arch and instep unsupported.

Hakes designed the shoe after studying footprints in sand and noticing that the heel and ball of the foot naturally support nearly all the weight of the wearer.

He set about designing a shoe as if he were designing a bridge, examining the forces in play and working out the simplest and most elegant way of providing the required support.

The result was a loop of carbon fibre laminated with rubber and leather for comfort. It resembled a twist of lime, which inspired the name Mojito.

Dezeen published the original green prototype in September 2009, triggering a viral frenzy that saw fashion bloggers, models and aficionados requesting a product that was still on the drawing board.

However a year later Hakes unveiled the first working prototypes at London Fashion Week and the shoe – by now made of a composite material – went into production in summer 2011.

Waste-to-Energy Plant
BIG

Leisure and industry do not usually co-exist in the same building but this power plant in Copenhagen doubles up as a winter sports centre.

The Waste-to-Energy Plant will generate electricity by incinerating waste, while its wedge-shaped roof will accommodate a 31,000 square metre ski slope. Skiers will be able to enjoy views across the city from a height of 100 metres as well as into the plant itself.

Designed by architects Bjarke Ingels Group (BIG), it was the winning entry in a competition launched by Danish waste management company Amagerforbrænding in 2010.

The plant's smokestack will emit a smoke ring whenever a tonne of carbon dioxide is released.

Minimal Dress
Digna Kosse

Design Academy Eindhoven graduate Digna Kosse wanted to make a statement about the clothing industry's voracious consumption of raw materials due to shifting fashion trends.

In an attempt to design fashionable, flattering clothes using the minimal amount of fabric, Kosse made 15 dresses in total, exploring different threads and techniques.

In the process she also created the second-most visited Dezeen story of all time, with over 175,000 visitors since we published it in October 2009. In general, despite the fact that Dezeen is an architecture and design site, any story featuring naked flesh tends to get good visitor figures.

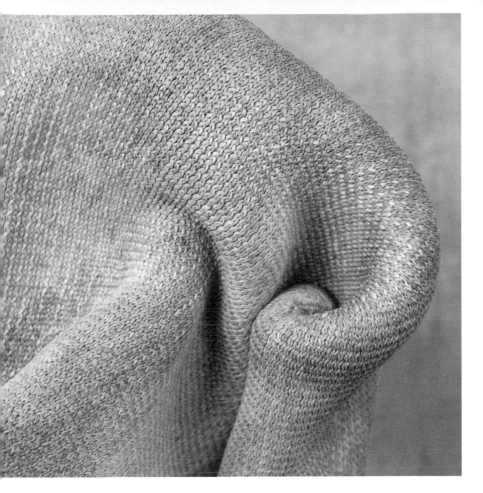

Concrete Cloth
Concrete Canvas

Concrete now comes on a roll. This flexible, concrete-impregnated fabric becomes rigid when sprayed with water; to use it you simply roll it out, manipulate it into shape and give it a good soaking.

Concrete Cloth remains malleable for two hours after it has been hydrated and reaches 80 per cent strength within 24 hours. When set, the concrete is thin, durable, waterproof and fire-resistant.

The cloth enables structures to be rapidly constructed without the need for heavy mixing equipment or moulds. Its applications range from disaster relief to civil engineering applications such as lining ditches and protecting pipes. It can also be used by architects to create decorative façades on buildings.

Manned Cloud
Jean-Marie
Massaud

Manned Cloud is a concept for a flying hotel that can accommodate up to 40 guests beneath a whale-shaped helium balloon.

Cruising at 130 kilometres per hour and with a top speed of 170 kilometres per hour, Manned Cloud would allow holidaymakers to experience some of the world's most beautiful places without being intrusive or exploitative.

The project suggests a return to the unhurried age of airship travel but with contemporary standards of hospitality: up to 15 members of crew would attend to passengers in the luxury two-level cabin, containing amenities including a restaurant, a library, a fitness suite and a spa.

There would also be a sundeck terrace on top of the balloon, which is accessed by lifts situated in between the double helium-filled envelopes. Three-day cruises would be on offer, covering up to 5,000 kilometres.

Conceived by French designer Jean-Marie Massaud, in collaboration with French aerospace research body ONERA, Manned Cloud was unveiled in 2008 and is still in development.

The airship is the third most popular story ever published on Dezeen, with over 170,000 visits since January 2008.

Structural Oscillations
Gramazio & Kohler

This 100-metre long brick wall was built entirely by a robot named R-O-B. The installation, by Swiss architects Gramazio & Kohler, consisted of 14,961 bricks arranged in an undulating loop around the Swiss Pavilion at the 11th Venice Architecture Biennale in 2008.

The architects designed R-O-B, a mobile fabrication unit, by adapting equipment typically used to assemble cars and perform other high-precision tasks, creating a machine that can accurately place bricks according to a digital program and in response to data about its surroundings. The oscillating wall resembled stretchy fabric rather than a solid structure and was assembled without the use of mortar.

The Venice installation, called Structural Oscillations, was the result of work by the Architecture and Digital Fabrication unit run by Gramazio & Kohler at the ETH University in Zurich. This ongoing research investigates the possibilities of full-scale digital fabrication: using industrial robots to construct buildings.

In 2009, R-O-B spent three weeks constructing a 22-metre long wall that weaved around a traffic island on Pike Street in New York. Pike Loop was built in collaboration with the NYC Department of Transportation's Urban Art Program and remained on show to the public for nearly a year before being dismantled. It was the first full-size architectural project in the USA to be built on site by an industrial robot.

Quinta Monroy
Alejandro Aravena
of Elemental

The budget for this social housing project in Chile wasn't big enough to provide the required 100 families with adequate houses, so instead the architects provided each of them with half a house.

Alejandro Aravena of Chilean architects Elemental was asked by the government to house the families, who had been illegally occupying the site at Quinta Monroy in Iquique. Yet the subsidy of approximately £5,000 per family was only enough to pay for the smallest housing type.

In response, the architects designed homes arranged in terraces where kitchens, bathrooms, stairs and limited living accommodation were provided using half of the available space. Residents were then left to fill in the remaining space in the voids between the houses themselves.

By gradually expanding their homes as and when they can afford it, the residents could end up with homes of 72 square metres, instead of the 30 square metres that the initial budget would have afforded.

Quinta Monroy was completed in 2004 but was published on Dezeen in 2008 after photographer Cristobal Palma visited the project and provided these images showing how residents had customised and added to their homes in the years since they had moved in.

Elastic House
Etienne Meneau

With a wobbly structure that flexes as waves pass beneath it, this concept for a house on a lake is designed to instill feelings of insecurity and nausea.

French Sculptor Etienne Meneau conceived the Elastic House as a refuge from the repetitive daily routines of life.

The Elastic House would require its inhabitants to have a strong stomach and a passion for being on the water. It is intended for those that like instability, feeling unsteady and being outdoors.

The natural rhythm and sounds would help to rebalance the people that escape to and spend time in the isolated structure.

Meneau wrote a poem to help explain his concept, translated here from French: 'When all goes well, when bore threatening, take your boat and go to live a while in your hut in the middle of a lake. Here you will recover instability: every wave becomes dangerous, even words must be weighed. And with a little luck, storm rising, everything will be swept away...'

Peepoo Bag
Anders Wilhelmson

The Peepoo Bag is a personal toilet that requires no water and converts human waste into a rich, harmless fertiliser within two to four weeks.

Launched in 2009, the single-use bag is designed primarily for informal settlements in the developing world, which often lack even the most rudimentary sanitation systems.

The user defecates or urinates directly into the Peepoo, which consists of a long, narrow outer bag and a wider inner layer of gauze that can be pulled out to increase the target area. The gauze also doubles as a substitute for toilet paper.

Once the top of the bag has been tied in a knot following use, it is safe to handle and can be stored or buried in the ground.

The inside of the bag is coated with urea powder, which starts to break down the contents and deactivate disease-producing organisms in the faeces. The process takes no more than a month, after which the resulting nitrogen-rich fertiliser can be safely handled.

The bag is made from degradable bioplastic, which itself eventually breaks down into carbon dioxide, water and biomass. Forty-five per cent of the plastic used to make the bag comes from renewable sources and Peepoople, the company behind the product, aims to eventually raise this to 100 per cent.

The bag was designed by Swedish architect Anders Wilhelmson in collaboration with Camilla Wirseen and Peter Thuvander.

Rolling Masterplan
Jägnefält Milton

Houses on wheels move freely around an abandoned network of industrial railway lines in this proposal for the regeneration of a Norwegian town.

The concept, by Swedish architects Jägnefält Milton, would allow people to shift their homes according to the season, moving to the lakeside in summer for example, or the town centre for festivals.

Rolling Masterplan consists of three standard rolling cabin sizes, all of which have a stove, bathroom and outer wood shell. Single Cabin has a multifunctional room with a foldaway king-sized bed, while Double Cabin has two rooms and is suitable for a family of four.

Suite has a living room, bathroom and bedroom over three floors, which are accessed by ladders fixed to the walls. The proposal also includes a hotel, swimming pool and concert hall.

The project was awarded third prize in an open international competition to design a new masterplan for the town of Åndalsnes in November 2010. The jury was impressed with the proposal's originality, focussing on using the existing railroad network rather than designing new city blocks and public squares.

Dezeen readers were excited by Rolling Masterplan and commented on its compelling and ethereal presentation imagery. Although it is feasible, readers highlighted logistical problems like receiving post and the need for sidetracks to allow cabins to overtake each other.

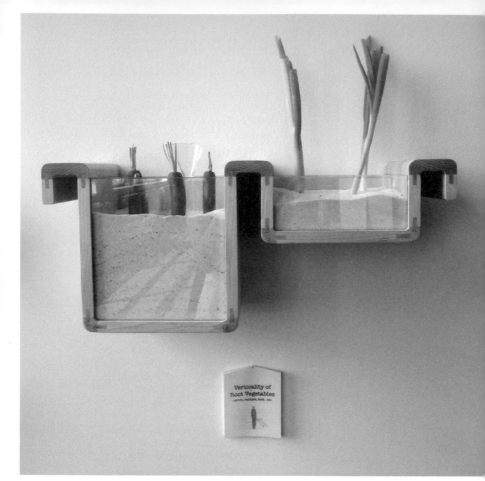

Shaping Traditional Oral Knowledge
Jihyun Ryou

Storing carrots in damp sand helps retain flavour, and keeping potatoes with apples prevents sprouting.

These are just two of the discoveries made by Jihyun Ryou during her investigation into food storage methods used before the advent of refrigeration. Ryou explored ways of reducing both the amount of food that is wasted and the quantity of energy used to preserve food in refrigerators.

She discovered that the brutally cold conditions in the fridge, where different produce is kept close together, could be detrimental to the flavour of many food types.

However, the lack of effort required to store food in the fridge meant that knowledge previously handed down from generation to

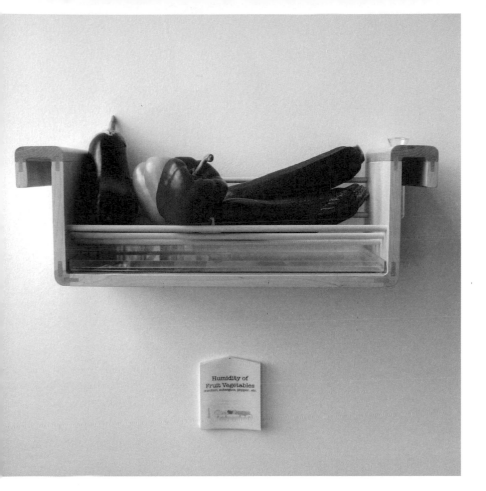

Humidity of
Fruit Vegetables
courgettes, aubergines, pepper, etc.

generation in different cultures
was in danger of being lost.

Shaping Traditional Oral
Knowledge, Ryou's graduation
project presented in 2009, was the
result of research into this
endangered wisdom. She presented
her findings as a series of wall-
mounted storage units under the
slogan: 'Save food from the fridge'.

The technique of storing carrots
and other root vegetables vertically
in moist sand (above left) comes

from her own Japanese ancestry.

Vegetables, such as courgettes,
which are strictly speaking fruit, are
best stored at room temperature
and kept moist, so Ryou designed a
shelf with a water trough beneath it
to humidify them (above right).

After discovering that the
ethylene gas emitted by apples
inhibits the sprouting of potatoes,
Ryou came up with an enclosed box
to keep potatoes in the dark with
holes on top where apples can sit.

FattyShell
Kyle Sturgeon, Chris Holzwart and Kelly Raczkowski

This experimental building method involves pouring concrete into a flexible rubber mould, to create bulging web-like structures that resemble fatty tissue.

The primitive, organic forms were produced using high-tech fabrication techniques developed by architecture students Kyle Sturgeon, Chris Holzwart and Kelly Raczkowski at the University of Michigan in 2010.

To make FattyShell (v.01), the students first used a robotic arm to precisely cut a series of holes in two large sheets of rubber. These membranes were then stitched together by another robot to create a stretchy mould.

The rubber formwork was attached to a plywood frame and tensioned at certain points with steel cables to create the curved structure. Plywood discs were also fixed to the rubber to control the internal depth of the mould.

Finally, fibre-reinforced concrete was poured into the void between the two membranes. This was done in 12 stages at three-hour intervals. Despite the staggered pouring, wet concrete continued to slide to the bottom of the formwork, causing the lower bulges.

Once the concrete was set, the rubber was cut away and the tension cables removed. The surface of the hardened concrete was marked by the seams and stitches that held the mould together.

Non-lethal Mousetraps Roger Arquer

Spanish designer Roger Arquer claims that he developed these mousetraps, 'only to catch mice, not to kill them'. It's doubtful that any of these flimsy contraptions would detain a rodent for long yet this remains one of the most popular stories we've published on Dezeen.

Arquer developed the idea as a student in 2005, but sent these photographs in two years later. The intention was not solely to catch mice without harming them, but to do so by only using readymade household objects such as pencils, bottles and paper clips.

There are four different design scenarios. Mouse in a Pint entails an inverted beer glass propped up by a breadstick attached to a spring. The mouse chews through the breadstick et voilà, it is trapped by the falling glass.

Mouse in a Bottle features a horizontal soy sauce bottle with a funnel-shaped spring in the neck. The mouse can squeeze in to reach the cheese, but is unable to escape.

Mouse in a Light Bulb (pictured) involves the glass part of a light bulb lying on its side, held by the weight of a metal nut. When the curious mouse steps inside, the bulb rights itself with the aperture at the top.

Mouse in a Planting Pot features a glass pot and a thin spring. The mouse climbs the spring, which bends under its weight, depositing the rodent inside, unable to escape.

While none of the traps are likely to take off, the exquisite sequences showing an obliging mouse (which is actually a gerbil) falling into the trap, make this a design based around an entertainingly conceptual notion of function, rather than function itself.

The Cloud
Atelier Hapsitus

Proposed in 2007 at the height of the construction boom in Dubai, The Cloud is a speculative design for a resort city elevated 300 metres in the air.

Supported on slanting tubular steel legs resembling rain, the city would be accessed via lifts housed in additional, non-slanting, tubes.

A 20,000 square metre platform on top of the columns would contain a pleasure park including a lake, gardens, rotating bridges, spiralling walkways and terraces, an auditorium and sports facilities.

The Cloud was developed by Nadim Karam of Beirut architects Atelier Hapsitus and presented to potential clients at the International Design Forum, a design conference held in Dubai in May 2007.

Around this time, architects from around the world were flocking to The Emirates to propose ever more daring projects. Other propositions included a hollow, spherical conference centre for Ras al Khaimah designed by Rem Koolhaas of OMA, which resembled the Death Star, and Jean Nouvel's opera house for Dubai that looked like an iceberg.

Within months, Dubai's real estate bubble had burst, leaving many projects half-built while dozens of the more ambitious schemes, such as The Cloud and those mentioned above, never got beyond the drawing board.

Brother Klaus Field Chapel Peter Zumthor

This chapel in Wachendorf, Germany was constructed from the inside out. And then set on fire.

The building process began with the construction of a teepee-like structure made of 112 tree trunks. Layers of concrete, each 50 centimetres thick, were gradually built up on top of the formwork over a period of 24 days.

Then a smoldering fire was created inside the chapel space in the autumn of 2006 to dry out the tree trunks. The fire was kept alight for three weeks, after which time the wood was removed, revealing a multi-faceted and highly grained wall surface.

Brother Klaus Field Chapel was designed by Swiss architect Peter Zumthor for a farmer and his wife, who carried out the majority of the construction with the help of friends and local craftspeople. The chapel is dedicated to Saint Nikolaus von der Flüe (1417–1487), who was known as Brother Klaus.

The building stands alone in the client's field, in the gentle mountainous region of Eifel. The solid exterior masks the curves of the richly textured interior, which is open to the sky (pictured).

Peter Zumthor was named Pritzker Prize Laureate in 2009, and Brother Klaus Field Chapel was among the projects cited by the jury.

Takasugi-an
Terunobu Fujimori

This eccentric Japanese teahouse on stilts was built by academic and architect Terunobu Fujimori.

Takasugi-an, which translates as 'a teahouse [built] too high,' consists of a single room perched on two chestnut tree trunks that were cut from a nearby mountain, in Chino, Nagano Prefecture.

It continues the tradition of teahouse construction by not using a skilled craftsman, which would be considered ostentatious. A freestanding ladder propped up against one of the trees provides access to the retreat, where guests have to remove their shoes before entering as per custom.

The serene interior is lined with plaster walls and bamboo mats and lacks the playfulness of the exterior, in order to create a calming environment appropriate for the art of making tea. A large window frames the view over Fujimori's hometown and his first building, Jinchokan Moriya Historical Museum. The window replaces the kakejiku, a picture scroll, hung to indicate the seasons.

Takasugi-an received lots of comments when Edmund Sumner's photographs were published on Dezeen in March 2009. Readers praised the adventurous vernacular design, and its refreshing contrast to modern architecture.

Another top ten post on Dezeen, this teahouse story has received over 155,000 visitors. See page 100 for another popular tree house story, The Mirrorcube in Sweden.

St. Bartholomew's Church
Maxim Velcovsky

When asked to refurbish a Baroque church in Eastern Bohemia, Czech designer Maxim Velcovsky dispensed with ecclesiastical norms. Instead he concocted a striking ensemble in which contemporary design classics, Bohemian crystal chandeliers and Mosque-style carpets are co-opted for religious use.

The nave of the church, in the village of Chodovice, had already been stripped of its accumulated layers of paint to reveal fragments of surviving decorative details, which were suggestive of the building's long history.

Working in 2007 with designer Jakub Berdych under the Qubus Studio banner, Velcovsky installed rows of white Verner Panton chairs,

each customised by punching a cross shape into the plastic backrest (above left). This act of tampering invalidated the warranty from manufacturer Vitra, but the designers felt it was worth the risk. Eames Plastic Side Chairs in white were specified for the clergy to sit at one end (above right).

Chandeliers have been hung along the nave and adorned with pressed and rough-cut crystal, while areas of the floor were covered by overlapping dozens of Persian carpets, in a manner more commonly found in a mosque.

Velcovsky's aim was not to shock, but to create a space in which the dialogue between objects from different design cultures might trigger wider cultural conversations within a religious environment.

NewspaperWood
Mieke Meijer
and Vij5

Unsold copies of newspapers can now be turned back into wood.

NewspaperWood is a material that has similar properties to timber. Sheets of newsprint are glued together to create logs, which are sawn into lightweight boards.

The boards can then be cut, milled and sanded just like real wood to make furniture, tableware and even jewellery. The individual layers of paper give the material a visible grain. Solvent-free glue is used so NewspaperWood could be recycled back into paper pulp.

Devised by Dutch designer Mieke Meijer with design studio Vij5, NewspaperWood is an example of 'upcyling' whereby low grade materials are converted into a higher-value material.

Gordon Wu CityLocal™ Aberrant Architecture

For the 2010 Hong Kong and Shenzhen Biennale of Urbanism and Architecture, Aberrant Architecture conceived an architectural hoax in the name of research. The London-based design studio and think tank set up a bogus trade stand to promote business products under the guise of a fictitious businessman, Gordon Wu.

One of the business models proposed was the Lunchbook (pictured), a mobile office canteen that tours residential areas so that people working from home can feel part of a big company community.

Other products included a set of lift doors, which can be installed inside the home to simulate a sense of arrival in the workplace, as well as a treadmill, complete with virtual businesspeople displayed on a screen, to imitate the experience of commuting to work.

As China continues to develop into a knowledge-based economy, working from home is increasing in popularity. The Gordon Wu CityLocal™ project seeks to tackle the sense of isolation and distraction associated with the home office. The franchises on offer focussed on bottom-up strategies for the city to develop in the future.

Ink Calendar
Oscar Diaz

Ink spilled on an absorbent surface will gradually spread via capillary action. Spanish designer Oscar Diaz harnessed this phenomenon to design a calendar in which the passing days of the month are marked by ink flooding across a series of connected numbers embossed on paper.

Diaz proposed bottles of ink in different colours for each month to represent fluctuations in temperature throughout the seasons, for example dark blue in December, shades of green during spring, and orange-reds in the summer months. The gradual progress of the ink is intended to provide a sensual, rather than a practical, measure of the passing of time.

The calendar was exhibited alongside other design pieces inspired by water at the Círculo de Bellas Artes in Madrid in summer 2009. It was originally developed for an exhibition called Gradual, which ran during London Design Festival two years earlier.

Ink Calendar is another of Dezeen's ten most popular stories and has been viewed by over 150,000 people.

Pewter Stool
Max Lamb

Rebuffed by sand-casting
foundries that laughed at his request
to produce a single stool, British
designer Max Lamb instead decided
to make it himself.

Lamb returned to a favourite
childhood beach in Cornwall and
sculpted the mould for his stool
directly into the wet sand.

The furniture designer melted
pewter – a malleable alloy consisting mainly of tin with small
amounts of copper and other metals
– in a saucepan placed on a camping
stove and poured the liquid metal
into the mould. Once it had cooled,
he dug away the sand to reveal the
finished product.

Despite being a comparatively
simple object, Pewter Stool is rich in
narrative. Tin mining was once the
main industry in Cornwall and sand

from local beaches was used in the casting foundries. The mould can only be used once, making each piece unique, and the unpredictability of working on a beach means that imperfections become an inevitable part of each object's charm.

The manufacturing process is imprecise and labour-intensive, yet practical considerations have driven the stool's design. The three-legged form ensures that it will not wobble even if, as often happens, the molten metal fails to flow to the bottom of the sand mould. The seat is a grid of tessellating triangles and allows the maximum sitting area from the minimum amount of pewter.

The stool is inseparable from the seaside performance that created it. Lamb produced a time-lapse movie of it being made. While the finished object has become a collectable rarity, the video documentary, disseminated on YouTube and Vimeo, is available to everyone.

Paper Rings
TT:NT

Thai designers Tithi Kutchamuch and Nutre Arayavanish have created a jewellery collection that is fragile, disposable and made of one of the cheapest materials they could find.

Their collection of twelve folded-paper rings together form a calendar, with one ring for each month. Each is inspired by the month's respective birth flower, ranging from a carnation for January to an orchid for December.

The flat-pack rings are laser engraved on one sheet of paper, and can be folded and assembled by the user at home. The rings are ephemeral precious objects, which might last just a few days and then be thrown away.

The origami-style jewellery was launched at the London Craft Fair, Origin, at Somerset House in 2008.

House in Buzen
Suppose
Design Office

Japanese architect Makoto Tanijiri
of Suppose Design Office is one of
Dezeen's biggest discoveries.
Practically unknown outside Japan
until recently, the prolific output of
unique private houses, retail
interiors and exhibition design from
this Hiroshima-based practice has

appeared regularly on our web
pages since 2009.

House in Buzen is the first of a
selection of four Suppose Design
Office projects in this book. Rooms
in the family home are conceived
like houses in a village, constructed
separately and linked by courtyards
and corridors that have glazed
roofs, creating outdoor-like spaces
where children can play, adults
can read and everyone can gather
to watch the stars at night.

House in Ekoda
Suppose
Design Office

The most striking feature of this renovated Tokyo apartment block by Suppose Design Office is the glazed conservatory on the roof, which has been converted into a bathroom with a view.

Completed in 2010, the bath, sink and toilet atop the three-storey building offer great views over the surrounding cityscape and are accessed by a wooden ladder that rises through a square hole cut in the floor, or by an external spiral staircase from the terrace below.

Elsewhere in the steel-framed building, the architects have removed walls and suspended ceilings to create three raw, open-plan apartments, into which faceted timber pavilions have been inserted that serve as bedrooms.

House in Nagoya
Suppose
Design Office

This house was built in 2009 for a client in Moriyama, in the city of Nagoya, who wanted a house with a vibrant garden on the plot he owned, which was tiny, narrow and surrounded by taller buildings.

To solve this issue, the architects devised a semi-submerged house with an internal underground garden. With one floor at ground level and one below, the house is built around a sunken courtyard. A void along one side of the kitchen allows extra natural light to reach the basement and provides additional planting space.

The feature that most intrigued Dezeen readers is the glazed toilet, which looks directly onto the garden and is in full view of the kitchen across the courtyard.

House in Koamicho
Suppose
Design Office

The fourth Suppose Design Office
project selected for this book has
once again played with the notion of
inside and outside at this house in
Hiroshima by creating garden
rooms. The two-storey concrete
building on a long narrow plot has
no windows but has instead been
divided up along its length into
three distinct blocks separated by
narrow glazed voids.

From the exterior, the voids
appear as horizontal stripes of glass
that wrap around the otherwise
featureless concrete hulk. The
cavities, which allow light into the
windowless rooms, are planted with
trees and shrubs on the ground floor
and crossed by metal bridges on the
upper floor.

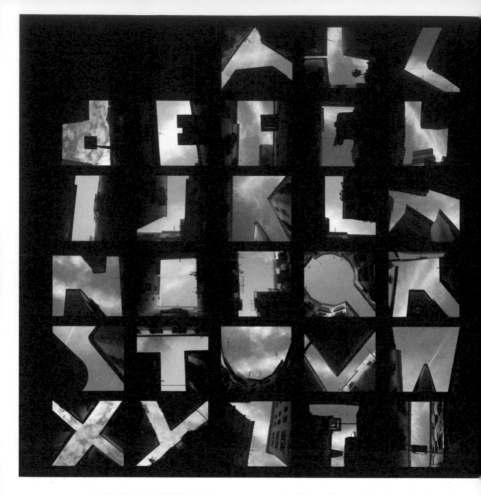

Type the Sky
Lisa Rienermann

By pointing her camera at the sky in urban streets, Lisa Rienermann has created a photographic alphabet of architectural letterforms.

The Berlin-based photographer began her odyssey while in Barcelona, where she stumbled across a tiny circular courtyard. Looking upwards, she noticed the buildings formed the letter Q when framed against the sky.

She subsequently embarked on a journey to seek out the 25 remaining letters in order to complete her Type the Sky alphabet. The more complicated letters such as Q and K were easiest to find, she says, but admits that Photoshop was required to complete some of the more elusive characters.

The project, which became a viral sensation when first published

online in 2007, relies on a counter-intuitive observation: seeing the sky as foreground and the buildings as background.

Type the Sky was part of Rienermann's thesis while studying at the University of Duisburg-Essen, where she presented it as a book. It won an award of Typographic Excellence from the Type Directors Club in New York in 2007.

The High Line
Field Operations
and Diller
Scofidio + Renfro

A long-abandoned elevated railway slicing through Manhattan has been transformed into a 1.5-mile long public park in one of the most successful urban transformations in recent years.

The High Line, which transported freight until the last train rolled through in 1980, traverses 22 blocks on the west side of Manhattan. Its rehabilitation as a linear park was led by landscape architects James Corner Field Operations in collaboration with architects Diller Scofidio + Renfro and garden designer Piet Oudolf.

Inspired by the way the disused piece of infrastructure was reclaimed by nature, the team proposed to retain its wild and strange beauty. They called their strategy 'agri-tecture', because it is part agriculture, part architecture.

The mixture of hard and soft landscaping varies along the line with some spaces that are completely paved and others richly planted. The landscaping strategy responds to distinct microclimatic zones that are variously sunny, shaded, wet, dry, windy and sheltered.

The paving consists of individual precast concrete planks with open joints that encourage the growth of wild grass. The High Line is being developed in three stages, each measuring one third of the total length. Phase I was completed in 2009 and phase II opened in 2011.

100 11th Avenue
Jean Nouvel

The ubiquitous glass curtain wall is usually flat and featureless but the curved façade of 100 11th Avenue in New York City features 1,650 panes of glass, each tilted at a different angle to neighbouring panes.

The result is a shimmering pixelated surface that dramatically fractures light in an ever-changing play of reflections.

The building's French architect, Jean Nouvel, calls it the 'vision machine' and claims that despite the simplicity of the idea, the curtain wall is the most complex ever built in the city.

The building, which sits on a corner site in Chelsea, is one of a rash of new apartment buildings by leading architects in New York, following a long period during which the city seemed to have lost interest in cutting-edge architecture.

Recent New York buildings published on Dezeen include New York by Gehry, a rippling 76-storey stainless steel tower by Frank Gehry that is the tallest residential tower in the western hemisphere, and Metal Shutter Houses by Shigeru Ban Architects, which features mesh roller shutters that cover the entire façade.

Finger-nose Stylus
Dominic Wilcox

'I am meeting with my nose,' said
Dominic Wilcox on Twitter when he
tested a new device. He had meant
to write, 'I am tweeting with my
nose,' but the message still proved
that it worked, more or less.

Wilcox came up with the idea for
a nose-mounted stylus after trying
to use his touch-screen phone in the
bath. He found that he put his
hand in the water without thinking,
rendering the phone unusable.

The prototype for a Finger-nose
Stylus is made of fibrous plaster
with a plastic stylus embedded in
the tip. The London-based designer
has found it surprisingly useful
outside the bath too, by allowing one
hand to remain free.

The design appeared on Wilcox's
website in April 2011 and quickly
received worldwide media coverage.

Motel Out of the Blue
Maartje Dros and Francois Lombarts

In the summer of 2009, while construction workers were on holiday, a building site in Amsterdam temporarily became a Spartan conference centre and hotel.

Designers Maartje Dros and Francois Lombarts transformed the concrete shell of the half-built apartment building into a venue for an experimental symposium on urbanism and hospitality. They used scaffold poles and rough wooden planks to furnish a meeting room, lecture hall, dining area and library, as well as sleeping accommodation for 50 people.

The designers took their inspiration from monasteries designed by Le Corbusier in the

1950s. Attendees sat on scaffold
pews and slept in cell-like bedrooms
that provided contemplative views
across IJburg, a new residential
suburb built on artificial islands in a
lake close to Amsterdam city centre.

Dros and Lombarts are both
graduates from Design Academy
Eindhoven, one of the design
schools that is most consistently
represented on Dezeen.

Public Space Shading Canopy Asif Khan, Omid Kamvari and Pavlos Sideris

Featureless streets where people have no reason to stop might become vital community spaces with the help of this simple kit.

A Public Space Shading Canopy kit contains everything required to erect an awning over a thoroughfare to provide shelter from the sun and rain. It differs from many of the ideas from architects for improving urban conditions as it is cheap and flexible, and can be erected by the community itself.

The idea was developed in 2007 by Architectural Association graduates Pavlos Sideris, Asif Khan and Omid Kamvari following a successful experience erecting a 15-metre long Lycra canopy in the Favela do Pilar slum in Recife, Brazil, in the previous year.

The yellow canopy was slung from telegraph poles and buildings using cables, and erected in just four hours with the help of locals.

According to the designers, this simple action immediately turned the neglected street into a vibrant public space as people stopped to linger in the shade and struck up conversation with one another.

The AA graduates produced the product in kit form for an exhibition called 'Design for the Other 90%' at the Cooper-Hewitt National Design Museum in New York City. It contains all the materials and tools that people would need to create their own canopies.

Incremental Housing Strategy Urban Nouveau*

This urban strategy for slum dwellers challenges the widespread belief that illegal shanties should be demolished and residents rehoused.

Working in Mumbai, India, architects Filipe Balestra and Sara Göransson of Urban Nouveau* developed an architectural model that allows residents to extend their homes as and when they can afford it, or with grant money from local authorities.

Balestra and Göransson were invited to India by the Society for the Promotion of Area Resource Centres (SPARC), an NGO that helps mobilise India's urban poor to improve their own living conditions.

The architects developed three simple housing prototypes for residents to choose from, all of which involve constructing basic concrete frames. Families start off living on the ground level, with the upper levels left unfinished.

Gradually these can be enclosed and inhabited, while there is the possibility for the ground floor to be turned into a shop or an office.

Incremental Housing Strategy, published in 2009, provides an alternative to simply uprooting victims of urban poverty, by instead helping them improve their communities organically.

The phenomenon of rapid urbanisation is creating what many believe is the world's biggest design problem: how to adequately house the millions of people who abandon the countryside each year to live in cities.

Sweeper Clock
Maarten Baas

Two janitors continuously sweep a large expanse of concrete as part of a 24-hour long performance by designer Maarten Baas. Pushing two lines of trash around with their brooms, the two men mark the time of day, with one pile of detritus advancing precisely every minute, and the other every hour.

The performance was recorded by a camera mounted overhead and went on for 12 hours non-stop to create a film that, when endlessly looped, functions as a clock.

Sweeper Clock was one of a series of time-based films created by Baas in 2009 as part of a project called Real Time. Shown on screens during the furniture fair in Milan, the films were also available for sale on digital hard drives that, when plugged into TV screens, turn into working timepieces.

Other elements of Real Time include Analog Digital Clock, a film in which a performer replicates a digital clock by painting over and wiping clean red panels on a black glass screen; and Grandfather Clock, which appears to feature a person inside an upright case repeatedly wiping off and drawing hands on the back of a glass clock face with a black pen.

The boundary between art and design has blurred in recent years with the rise of the limited edition, gallery-driven collectors market, yet Baas insists that the functional nature of these films – the fact that they tell the time – grounds them firmly in the world of design.

The Mirrorcube
Tham & Videgård
Arkitekter

Tourists looking for unusual accommodation in Lapland, northern Sweden, can now stay in a mirrored glass cube perched up a pine tree.

The Mirrorcube, designed by Swedish architects Tham & Videgård, was built in 2010 as part of Treehotel, which is located in a forest close to the Arctic Circle near the village of Harads. The hotel features six tree house retreats by different designers that allow guests to get close to nature.

The Mirrorcube has a lightweight aluminum structure attached to the tree trunk, which passes through the centre of the room. Transparent ultraviolet film is laminated onto the reflective glass panes to prevent birds colliding with it.

A rope bridge provides access to the cube, which sleeps two people. The interior is made of plywood and has a series of square windows that provide 360-degree views of the surrounding landscape.

The cube contains a double bed, small bathroom, living room and a roof terrace (see image on the following page). »

» Other rooms at Treehotel include The Bird's Nest, The Cabin and The UFO. The Bird's Nest, designed by Inredningsgruppen, is a cylindrical room featuring an exterior clad in a casing of twisted branches. The interior, by contrast, is timber-clad and minimal. The hotel room is reached via a retractable staircase.

The UFO, also designed by Inredningsgruppen, is a disc-shaped spaceship with a composite shell and porthole windows that hangs among the branches. The Cabin by Cyrén and Cyrén is a rectangular structure similar to a shipping container lodged among trees above a steep slope and accessed by a gantry.

The hotel also features the drum-shaped Tree Sauna, which is raised off the ground in a clearing and accessed by an external spiral staircase.

Melissa + Gaetano shoe
Gaetano Pesce

These ankle boots can be converted into personalised shoes by snipping away some of the moulded plastic discs with scissors.

Italian architect Gaetano Pesce designed the footwear for Melissa, a Brazilian shoe brand specialising in moulded plastic 'jelly' shoes.

Melissa + Gaetano is one of a range of collaborations between the brand and leading architects and designers, including Zaha Hadid and Jean-Paul Gaultier, but this was the first to offer customers the chance to customise their purchase.

The shoes, released in 2010, can be converted into different styles according to the owner's preference.

Switch
Yuko Shibata

A sliding wall in a small Tokyo apartment transforms the dining room into a meeting room and separate library.

When in dining room mode, the wall conceals a floor-to-ceiling bookcase. This is revealed when the partition is slid into the room, dividing the space in two. A large rectangle cut out of the wall allows it to pass over the top of the dining table, meaning the table can be used in both the office and the library at the same time.

Called Switch, and completed in 2010, the apartment was designed by Japanese architect Yuko Shibata, who created a flexible space where the owners can work, study and hold meetings without interrupting their home life.

A second ingenious feature in the apartment is a hinged panel in the bedroom that swings open to reveal a brightly painted study consisting of a bookshelf with a built-in seating alcove. When open, the panel conceals the bed from the study, allowing one person to work without disturbing their sleeping partner. When closed, all that is visible is a plain timber screen.

Rolex Learning Centre
SANAA

Resembling a fairground waltzer in glass and steel, this university building in Switzerland has sloping floors instead of stairs, and wide flowing spaces instead of walls and narrow corridors.

From the air, the Rolex Learning Centre in Lausanne looks like a square slice of bumpy Swiss cheese, dotted with holes and peeling off the ground in places.

The 20,000 square metre interior is conceived as one huge room, devoid of walls, doors and steps, and undulating like a carpeted landscape of gentle hills. The concrete ceiling is kept floating by the most slender of steel columns and the perimeter is seamlessly glazed, as are the voids that pierce the building to allow light to enter.

Designed by Japanese architects SANAA and opened in 2010, the centre is located on the campus of the Ecole Polytechnique Fédérale de Lausanne (EPFL) and hosts a range of learning resources including a library and study areas, plus cafes and restaurants.

The radical treatment of the interior is designed to break down conventions that cause people to behave one way in the classroom and a different way in the corridor.

By introducing slopes of varying steepness, the architects have given the students the chance to find new ways of using their surroundings.

Dezeen readers were particularly intrigued as to whether skateboarding was allowed in the building.

Over 10,000 researchers and students are based on the campus, which overlooks Lake Geneva and the Alps and is one of the world's leading institutions for engineering technology and computer sciences.

Baked
Formafantasma

These objects for storing food are themselves made of food.

Flour mixed with ingredients including coffee, spinach, cocoa, salt and spices have been used to create the Baked collection of containers and vessels by Andrea Trimarchi and Simone Farresin of Studio Formafantasma.

The Italian designers, who both studied at Design Academy Eindhoven in the Netherlands, presented the collection at Dutch Design Week in 2009, taking their inspiration from the Feast of San Giuseppe festival at Salemi, Sicily, where a flour-based material is used to produce architecturally themed table decorations.

The following year Trimarchi and Farresin developed the idea further, presenting a collection of pots, lamps and tools composed of 70 per cent flour, 20 per cent agricultural waste and 10 per cent limestone. Called Autarky, the collection is inspired by the idea of a hypothetical rural community who derive all their food, tools and utensils from the land around them.

In 2011, Studio Formafantasma took their investigations further still with Botanica, a range of vases, lights and furniture. The designers extracted polymers from resin, shellac, rubbers, wood and animal products to make natural plastics.

The organic forms, derived from seedpods and pinecones, hark back to a time before the advent of oil-based polymers, when naturally derived plastics were considered materials of the future.

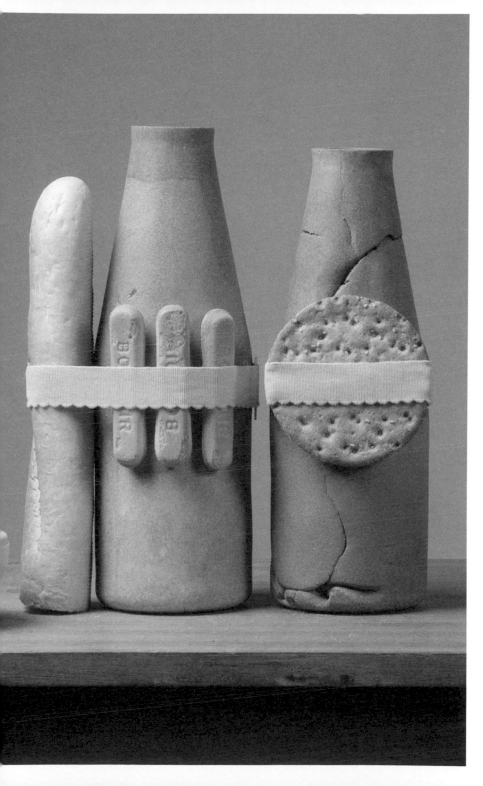

Eco-friendly Phone
Daizi Zheng

The juice to power this mobile phone comes, literally, from juice.

Instead of a standard battery, the proposal by Chinese designer Daizi Zheng features a bio-battery fuelled by a sugar-rich solution contained in a screw-top glass tube.

Enzymes in the battery convert the sugar into electricity via an electrochemical reaction. The solution could be a mixture of sugar and water, fruit juice or any commercial fizzy drink. To charge the phone, the user simply tops up the tube.

Zheng proposed the Eco-friendly Phone concept – which is not yet commercially viable but still theoretically possible – while studying at Central Saint Martins in London. It was in response to a brief from Finnish brand Nokia that called for a more sustainable way of powering mobile phones.

Standard phone batteries are expensive to produce and cause pollution both during their manufacture and disposal. They also consume mains electricity each time they are charged.

By contrast, the only waste created by the Eco-friendly Phone is the by-products of the chemical reaction: water and oxygen.

Plytube
Seongyong Lee

It seems an obvious idea but nobody has done it before: Korean designer Seongyong Lee has invented a way of making wooden cylinders.

Lee adapted industrial processes normally used in the production of cardboard tubes, using wooden veneers instead of paper. The thin layers of timber are wrapped obliquely and glued to create an extremely strong, lightweight material called Plytube.

He developed the idea while studying at the Royal College of Art in London, where he also developed techniques for joining the tubes together using traditional wood-working tools.

Plytube was used to make a series of extremely lightweight, handcrafted furniture for Lee's graduation show in 2010. The stools and side tables demonstrate the material's properties; each of the small stools can support the weight of an adult yet weighs just 820 grams. When used as a table, the hollow core of the tubes can be used as a channel for cables for a computer or lamp.

Furniture made of Plytube requires far lower quantities of wood than items made of solid timber. The tubes can be made from low-grade timber and offcuts, making it a highly sustainable material. The manufacturing process could potentially be scaled up to produce architectural components.

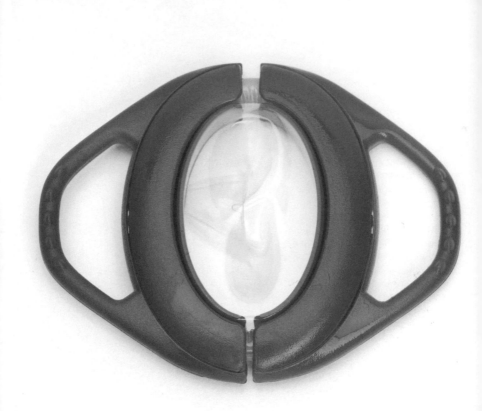

4:Secs Condoms ...XYZ

As the punning name suggests, these condoms can be applied rapidly thanks to an integrated applicator that allows the contraceptive to be pulled over the penis in one swift movement.

The applicator consists of a plastic ring that holds the condom with finger-and-thumb grips on each side. When the condom is fully unrolled, the ring snaps in two and can be discarded.

Relaunched in 2008, it was the invention of Willem van Rensburg and developed by South African designers ...XYZ in an attempt to encourage people to use condoms and prevent HIV transmission.

By making condoms quicker and easier to apply, the designers hope to remove some of the stigma attached to their use.

See Better to Learn Better
Yves Behar

Mexican children with poor eyesight get free designer spectacles under an initiative funded by the Mexican government.

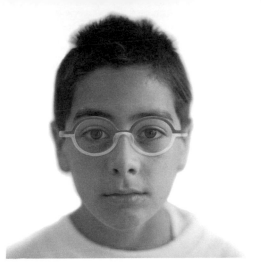

The glasses, designed by San Francisco industrial designer Yves Behar, are distributed annually and free of charge to pupils aged 6-18 years old who cannot afford prescription lenses. The Ver Bien para Aprender Mejor (See Better to Learn Better) project responds to research that found that the academic performance of children from disadvantaged families in Mexico drops significantly as they progress through the education system, largely due to bad eyesight.

The virtually unbreakable mix-and-match spectacle frames are designed to overcome the social stigma associated with wearing glasses. Children are given an eye examination at school before choosing their frames, which are available in seven colours, five shapes and three sizes. The options are displayed in an interactive flip chart book that builds anticipation and excitement around the glasses.

The frames are made of flexible Gilamid plastics, the lightest engineering plastics currently available, so they can be worn during sports. The glasses are produced by Mexican manufacturer Augen Optics.

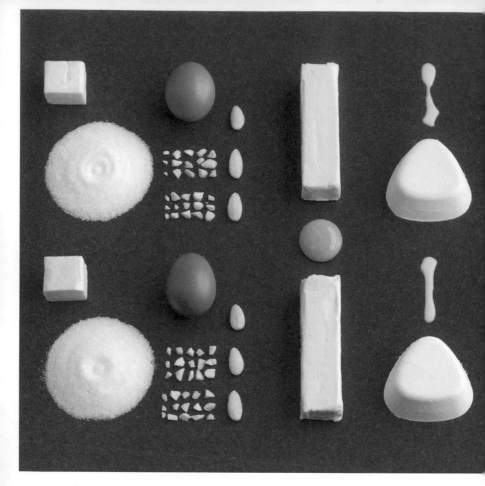

Homemade is Best Forsman & Bodenfors for IKEA

Homeware brand IKEA is known for flat-pack furniture sold with step-by-step assembly instructions. When the company commissioned a recipe book in 2010, the designers applied the same principle to the assembly of food.

The 140-page coffee-table book contains 30 classic recipes for Swedish cakes and biscuits including gingerbread people, pastries and fruit tarts. All are brought to life with photographs of the ingredients arranged in abstract compositions on a brightly coloured background.

Called Homemade is Best and designed by Swedish creative agency Forsman & Bodenfors, the project was part of a larger marketing campaign to generate consumer

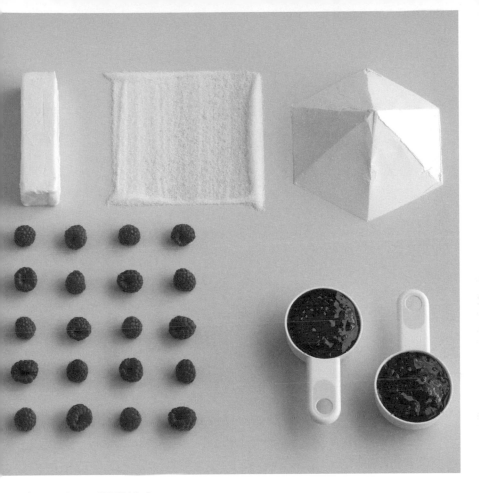

interest in new IKEA kitchens
and kitchen appliances.

Forsman & Bodenfors collaborated with photographer Carl Kleiner
and stylist Evelina Bratell to create
the series of images inspired by
contemporary fashion and Japanese
minimalism. Each recipe is
presented on a double-page spread,
followed on the next page by a
picture of the finished dish.

Dezeen readers loved the concept
but were disappointed not to be »

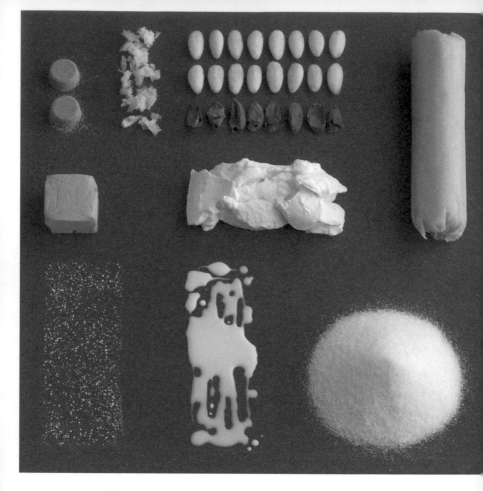

» able to purchase a copy as it was only available in Sweden.

Opinion was divided between readers who thought that it should include the written recipes so that it is useable for baking, and those that argued it to be a stronger and purer idea without.

However our original story gave the misleading impression that there were no words in the book — an error that was copied by many of the other websites that followed up the story. The book did in fact include written instructions explaining how to make all the items depicted.

Homemade is Best won the Brit Insurance Graphics Award 2011.

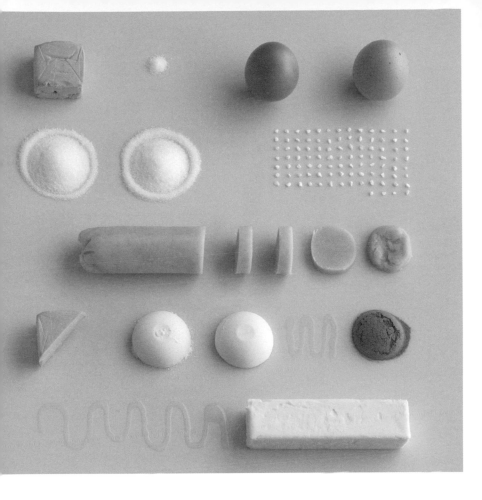

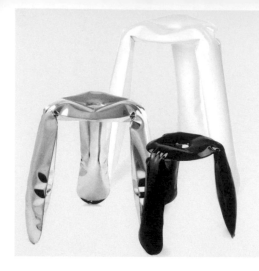

Plopp Stool
Oskar Zieta

This stool is made in the same way as an inflatable beach toy, only from stainless steel instead of plastic.

Initially produced in 2008, it was the first commercial product made using a revolutionary new manufacturing process invented by Polish designer Oskar Zieta.

To make the stool, two sheets of ultra thin stainless steel are laser cut into the outline of the flattened stool, which are then welded together along their edges.

This creates a flat, airtight form, which is inflated under high pressure using compressed air. The steel deforms under the pressure, creating a three-dimensional object with great structural stability.

The manufacturing process, called FiDU, was developed in Zurich at the Swiss Federal Institute of Technology, where Zieta teaches. The technique has many advantages. It is relatively cheap, since only a minimum amount of stainless steel is required for each object and the inflating process requires only a standard air compressor. The stools can be flat-packed for shipping, and inflated at their destination.

Following the stool, Zieta has gone on to create an ever-expanding range of objects using the technique, and has experimented with other materials including copper and aluminium. Since FiDU produces an extremely high strength-to-weight ratio, research is underway to adapt the technique to structural applications such as bridges and even buildings.

Move: Choreographing You exhibition Amanda Levete Architects

A giant folded paper-like ribbon meandered through an exhibition about performance art, resembling the flowing robes of a dancer. By rising and falling, it divided up the galleries and guided visitors through the exhibits.

The exhibition design for Move: Choreographing You, held at the Hayward Gallery in London in 2010, featured no solid walls or display cabinets, instead consisting solely of origami structures suspended from the ceiling.

London practice Amanda Levete Architects collaborated with Kite Related Design to design the exhibition, taking inspiration from choreography, which begins as something geometric but evolves into fluid movement.

The spatial dividers captured the blur of a dancer moving through the air, and encouraged fluid navigation around the interactive exhibition. At points, the folded structure lifted to allow people to pass from one exhibit to another; at other points, it enclosed more intimate spaces.

The material used for the dividers is Tyvek, a translucent synthetic fabric made of spun polyethylene fibres, which can be folded like paper but which is resistant to tearing.

Safe House
Robert
Konieczny

Designed for an extremely
security-conscious client, this house
transforms itself from an open, airy
villa by day into an impenetrable
fortress by night.

The rectangular concrete house
sits in a large garden close to a high
perimeter wall and, when in open

mode, features large windows
and a double-height glass wall.
A drawbridge connects the
first floor to the adjoining building,
which contains a swimming pool
and a roof terrace. There is a secure
place for children to play within
a walled courtyard.

At night, however, the house
changes both form and appearance,
morphing into a windowless
monolith. The courtyard walls – one
of which is 15 metres long and the

other, 22 metres long – slide back on rollers to shield the ground floor of the house. A massive aluminium shutter, measuring fourteen by six metres, and made by a company that normally supplies shipyards, unrolls to completely cover the expansive glass wall.

The drawbridge raises to conceal the first-floor entrance and huge hinged steel panels, each 2.8 metres high, fold back to block out the remaining windows.

The house, located in a village on the outskirts of Warsaw, was designed by Polish architect Robert Konieczny and completed in 2009.

Chairless
Alejandro Aravena

Rather than being a chair, this product is a 'a simple tool for sitting'. It consists of a fabric strap that loops around your back and knees to stabilise and alleviate pressure while sitting on the ground in a cross-legged position.

Chairless was designed in 2010 by Alejandro Aravena for the furniture brand Vitra. The Chilean architect observed that people sit in order to relieve tension in their backs, rather than their legs, proven by the fact that people can walk for longer than they can stand still.

Weighing 85 grams, the strap can be folded up and put in a pocket.

The design is based on a sitting strap used for generations by the nomadic Ayoreo tribe who live in the Gran Chaco border region between Paraguay and Bolivia.

Christmas Cards Heatherwick Studio

The Christmas cards sent out by Thomas Heatherwick of Heatherwick Studio each year are as ingenious as his design and architecture projects.

Since 1996, the London-based designer has created cards that are miniature marvels of paper engineering or sculpture, each playing on the theme of postage.

The stamps used to pay for the cards' carriage often play a central role in the design. 2004's design featured hand-franked red one-penny stamps glued together to form a Christmas tree decoration. The 2009 edition was a Christmas tree-shaped latex mould of the front of a classic British red postbox while the 2010 version was an assembly of 24 tiny envelopes that formed an advent calendar.

Alas, new Royal Mail postal rates have made it ever more expensive to send out unusual-sized packages and Thomas Heatherwick has hinted that the 2010 edition might have been the last.

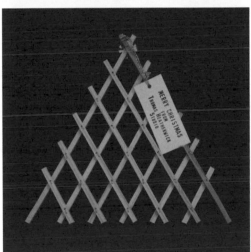

MD.net Clinic Akasaka
Nendo

False doors, walls that open and sliding bookshelves are among the design features at this psychiatric clinic in Akasaka, Japan.

The interior expresses the client MD.net's innovative approach to 'total mental healthcare', which focusses on enriching patients' daily lives and providing alternative ways of viewing the world.

Looking more like a comfortable gentlemen's club than the average sterile healthcare facility, the clinic is designed to prevent clients – who include people who want to return to the workplace and corporate clients – feeling intimidated.

The space is full of quirky details including consulting rooms that are accessed by hidden panels in the walls, a sliding door disguised as a bookcase, and windows concealed behind doors.

Opened in 2010 and designed by Japanese designers Nendo, the interior caused much discussion on Dezeen over the appropriate nature of such a strong design statement for a psychiatric facility.

125

Illoiha Omotesando Climbing Wall
Nendo

Another quirky interior by Nendo. This time, an indoor climbing wall that looks less like the usual artifical rockface and more like a stately home. The eccentric wall features climbing holds in the form of deer heads, picture frames, mirrors, birdcages and vases.

The Illoiha Omotesando fitness club is located within a two-storey basement in the Omotesando fashion district, where the clientele is more likely to be stylish urbanites than rugged outdoor types.

Both the gym and wall were designed by the Japanese designers in 2006 and judging by the comments posted by Dezeen readers, they have achieved their aim of enticing newcomers to try out rock climbing.

iPad
Apple

We could hardly write a book about design ideas without including an Apple product.

When Dezeen launched in November 2006, neither the iPhone nor the iPad existed. Today it's hard to imagine life without them.

Apple CEO Steve Jobs unveiled the iPad – a touch-screen device for browsing the internet, watching films, reading e-books and playing games – at the beginning of 2010.

It employed the high-resolution display technology of the iPhone, which automatically switches from portrait to landscape as the device is turned. The hotly anticipated product was thinner and lighter than any laptop.

Comments from Dezeen readers were initially sceptical, with one saying it looked like a digital photo frame and another dubbing it the 'iPhone stretch'.

The iPad, however, was soon accepted as a genuinely new product type, with some publishing industry executives seeing app-based subscriptions as a potential salvation for business models that had been severely eroded by websites offering free content.

As a physical object, the design of the iPad is an exercise in demateri-alisation: it does away with hardware such as the keyboard, the mouse and anything else that might detract from the one essential feature – the screen.

The design genius lies in the intuitive multi-touch interface, and the countless apps that have been developed to run on the iPad.

Oogst 1 Solo
Tjep.

Oogst, meaning 'harvest' in Dutch, is a series of proposals by Amsterdam-based designers Tjep. for farms that could provide inhabitants with everything they require.

The high-tech farms generate energy, heat, oxygen and food as well as processing their own waste, making them entirely self-suffi-

cient. Each would mimic a natural ecosystem, requiring only wind and solar energy for power.

There are three concepts, which each support a different number of people; Oogst 1 Solo is for a single person (pictured). They stand clear of the ground and could be placed on top of existing buildings.

The project stimulates thought about how cities can support larger populations without increasing consumption of natural resources.

Jar Tops
Jorre van Ast

Jar Tops is a range of polypropylene lids that transform used food jars into shakers, sprinklers and pourers. They screw onto glass jars that would otherwise be thrown away to create a highly personal collection of storage utensils.

The designs started life as a student project by Dutch designer Jorre van Ast, who first exhibited the collection in 2006 at his Royal College of Art graduation show.

They were later put into production by Dutch kitchenware manufacturers Royal VKB, who now sell them in packs of five: a sugar shaker, a jug for milk or water, a cocoa sprinkler and an oil and vinegar set.

Jars Tops have also made it into the permanent collection at New York's Museum of Modern Art.

Local River
Mathieu
Lehanneur

Part aquarium, part vegetable garden and part domestic ornament, this project takes cutting-edge agricultural techniques and puts them in your living room.

Local River by French designer Mathieu Lehanneur is a domestic adaptation of aquaponics, an ancient technique whereby nutrient-rich fish waste is used to fertilise crops. The concept would allow people to breed freshwater fish for eating and grow vegetables, all within the home.

Agriculturalists have only recently adapted the principle to create sustainable farming systems that combine hydroponics (growing plants in water instead of soil) with aquaculture (farming fish in tanks). The plant roots absorb waste excreted by the fish, filtering and purifying the water in the process.

Local River takes its visual cues from contemporary art and design. It features a number of sculptural hand-blown glass plant pots mounted on rectilinear fish tanks. The pots are used to grow lettuce and other fast-growing crops.

The project is a response to consumer demands for more sustainable farming methods, and in particular the 'locavores' – a movement born in San Francisco that believes in only eating food grown within a 100-mile radius.

Lehanneur developed Local River in conjunction with Anthony van den Bossche and first exhibited it at the Artists Space Gallery in New York in 2008.

Workshop Chair
Jerszy Seymour

No tools or specialist skills are required to make the Workshop Chair. The maker only needs to have enough hand-eye coordination to join timber batons together with blobs of polycaprolactone wax.

The chair was designed in 2009 around the notion of an amateur society, whereby unskilled people could produce items of furniture every bit as functional as those by professionals. Jerszy Seymour's notion of the amateur is based on its etymology, meaning 'lover of'.

The Workshop Chair's ungainly form is deceptive; the waxy blobs create joints that are strong enough to pass the structural tests for contract office furniture. The wax is a biodegradable polyester. When molten, the material can be manipulated and applied by hand.

Seed Cathedral
Heatherwick
Studio

Surrounded by a hairy fuzz instead of solid walls, the UK Pavilion at Shanghai Expo 2010 became known in China as The Dandelion.

The nebulous façade was composed of 60,000 fibre-optic rods, each 7.5 metres long, which pierced the pavilion's timber superstructure. During the day, the rods drew light into the interior while at night they transmitted light out, causing the building to glow.

Heatherwick's pavilion showcased the work of the Kew Millen-nium Seed Bank in London, which houses the largest collection of wild plant seeds in the world. A different seed was embedded in the tip of each of the transparent rods.

Seed Cathedral won gold in the design category at the Expo.

12 Blocks
Loom Studio

Loom Studio has rethought one of the most familiar components in architecture: the concrete block. The Minnesota architects propose 12 variations on the standard block, modifying the outer face with a range of simple sculptural flourishes that, when laid together to make a wall, would create dramatically different patterns.

The idea, developed as part of a research project, was driven by concern over the increasing standardisation of building materials. While making components cheaper, this is also leading to less variety in buildings.

The architects recognised that the standard American concrete masonry unit, or CMU, had remained unchanged for decades, and so developed the 12 Blocks to propose ways of introducing greater diversity to the streetscape.

The new blocks could be manufactured by making simple adaptations to the steel forms that are used to mould CMUs, meaning they could be made on existing production lines.

Concrete blocks are usually manufactured as close to the construction site as possible and Loom Studio also proposed that CMU plants use a percentage of locally sourced minerals such as clay, volcanic ash or even coal, rice husks from agriculture or discarded shells from the fishing industry.

These variations could therefore create strong regional identities in construction projects that would otherwise be bland.

National Glass Museum
Bureau SLA

When asked to refurbish two detached villas for a museum, one for public use and one for staff, Dutch architects Bureau SLA left the vernacular houses alone but linked each of their four storeys with dramatic bridge-like corridors that cross in mid-air.

The result is a surreal hybrid of the old and the new. The corridors, clad in polycarbonate panels behind aluminium mesh, double as exhibition spaces that display over 9,000 objects in glass cabinets, and glow at nighttime. The two original villas effectively act as one building now, with one containing a restaurant and the other, a library.

The National Glass Museum at Leerdam in the Netherlands opened in 2010.

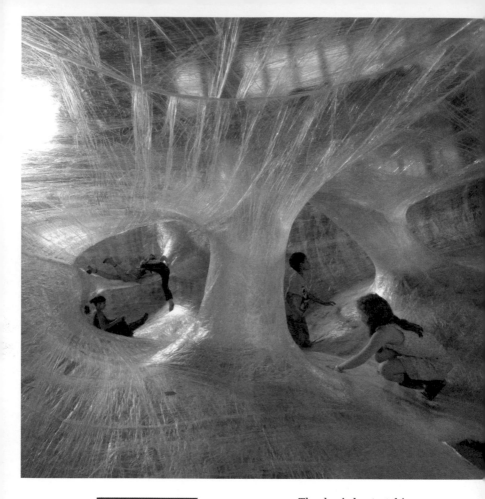

Tape Berlin
Numen / For Use

Sticky tape becomes an
architectural material capable of
forming inhabitable cocoon-like
structures in the hands of designers
Numen / For Use.

The designers use hundreds of
rolls of transparent tape to create
installations that are strong enough
for people to climb inside.

They begin by stretching
tendon-like lengths of tape between
points in the host building to create
a grid over which tape is wrapped in
layers to create an organic web. Each
installation takes several days to
complete and consumes up to 50
kilometres of tape.

The idea for the tape installations
evolved from a set-design brief for a
dance show where dancers trailed
tape behind them as they moved
between columns, leaving behind a

record of their movements. Since the first installation between the beams of a Viennese attic in 2009, the designers have built layered transparent passageways between the historic pillars of a former stock exchange in Vienna and the 1980s columns at the entrance to the Schirn Kunsthalle in Frankfurt.

With each installation, the forms become more complex and suggestive of new architectural possibilities.

The installation shown here was created as part of the DMY Berlin design show in 2010, held at Tempelhof airport in Berlin. Tape was stretched from a specially erected scaffolding structure.

Numen / For Use was founded by Sven Jonke, Christoph Katzler and Nikola Radeljkovic and has offices in Vienna and Zagreb. The designers divide their activities between product design, and exhibitions, installations and set design.

Masdar Initiative
Foster + Partners

A cluster of sand-coloured buildings in the Abu Dhabi desert mark the start of one of the most ambitious sustainable developments ever conceived – the world's first 'zero carbon, zero waste' city.

The campus buildings for the Masdar Institute research facility, completed in 2010 (top image), form the first phase of Masdar City.

Plans unveiled in 2007 – but subsequently scaled back – showed a six million square metre urban quarter based on the planning principles of a walled city (bottom image), with narrow pedestrian streets, shaded courtyards and buildings screened by mashrabiya – projecting windows covered with decorative perforated panels.

The city, masterplanned by architects Foster + Partners, would generate all its electricity from solar panels, it was announced. Cars would be banned, with inhabitants instead moving around in driverless electric pods guided by magnetic strips embedded in the ground.

The first completed phase generates a surplus of electricity, which is fed back into the grid. The architects claim the buildings consume 54 per cent less water and 51 per cent less electricity than average in this part of the world.

Buildings feature projecting façades and overhanging photo-voltaic panels to increase shading in the pedestrian alleys. The glass-reinforced concrete panels used to clad the buildings are mixed with local sand to help them blend in with the landscape.

Air Multiplier
Dyson

Serial inventor James Dyson has turned his attention to the desktop fan, producing a bladeless design that is windier, safer and easier to clean, and which produces a continuous stream of air.

The Air Multiplier, which came out in 2009, has a motor in its base, which reverses the top-heavy awkwardness of conventional blade fans. This drives air upwards into a hollow ring where it accelerates through a narrow aperture and passes over an airfoil-shaped ramp.

The resulting jet of air draws in more air from outside the fan, multiplying the total volume of air being expelled by 15 times and giving the product its name.

With no rotating blades to slice the air, the fan produces a constant flowing breeze, rather than a choppy one, and is consequently quieter in the process. The device features a dimmer control to precisely adjust the wind power, and a magnetic remote control that sticks to the fan so it doesn't get lost.

In 2010, Dyson added a pedestal version of the desk fan to the range as well as a tower design, which has an elongated loop instead of a circular head.

Casas na Areia
Aires Mateus
Architects

You don't need to worry about getting the sand off your feet when entering these holiday homes in Portugal, as the floor is an extension of the beach. And you don't need to worry about the evening chill, because a heating system embedded in the sand keeps it warm.

The Casas na Areia, meaning 'houses in the sand', sit within a 12,000-hectare wildlife sanctuary near the fishing village of Comporta, one hour south of Lisbon.

Architects Aires Mateus designed the buildings to integrate with the coastal landscape, with walls and roofs made from natural wattle and bulrush. The development, completed in 2010, consists of a cluster of four thatched huts that sleep a total of eight visitors. Paths of wooden boards laid on the sand link the huts together.

The sand continues into two timber-framed huts, housing a kitchen and living space. The two other huts are masonry structures that each contain two double bedrooms. With grey, polished concrete floors and white Corian bathroom fixtures, the bedrooms are the only sand-free zones in the accommodation.

Rapidprototyped-shoe
Marloes ten Bhömer

Even the most uncomfortable-looking shoes would fit perfectly if footwear was made using 3D printing technology.

Dutch designer Marloes ten Bhömer created the experimental Rapidprototypedshoe using this technology in 2010 for Mechanical Couture: Fashioning a New Order at the Design Museum Holon in Israel. The exhibition explored the role of machines and technology in redefining fashion.

3D printing, also known as rapid prototyping, allows objects to be made in one piece, instead of being assembled from multiple components, thereby permitting far more complex forms than would otherwise be possible.

Shoes made this way could be produced according to the precise dimensions of the wearer's feet and would have none of the imperfections of a hand made shoe.

Rapidprototypedshoe is made by layering photopolymer materials, which are then UV cured. Even though the shoe is made in one stage, rather than many, separate parts can be replaced if they wear out first.

Paper Eyelashes
Paperself

False paper eyelashes featuring horses and deer are an unlikely idea for a design product, but they have been remarkably successful.

These delicate accessories are inspired by the art of Chinese paper cutting and were created by Paperself, a collective started by London designer Chunwei Liao.

They come in two sizes – one a full eyelash and one just for corners – and 11 styles that reference traditional Chinese symbols. These include peach blossom as a symbol of romance, horses that stand for success, and butterflies, which represent freedom and beauty.

The lashes were one of the best-selling products at The Temporium, a designer Christmas market co-organised by Dezeen in London's Brompton Road in 2010.

Flooded London
Squint/Opera

Scenarios predicting the future
effects of climate change tend to be
apocalyptic, but London film studio
Squint/Opera paints a rosier picture
in this series of images that imagine
London in 2090, after it has been
inundated by rising sea levels.

The Flooded London project
depicts a post-catastrophic city that

has come to terms with its new
circumstances. The remaining
inhabitants enjoy the tranquillity
afforded by half-submerged
monuments and abandoned
districts in a manner reminiscent
of the way nineteenth-century
travellers experienced the neglected
sights of antiquity.

One image features a man in
swimming trunks preparing to dive
off a ledge in the Whispering
Gallery, high up in the dome of St

Paul's Cathedral (above left). It is
as if he were a holidaymaker getting
ready to leap into a jungle stream.

Other images feature people
fishing from derelict office
skyscrapers, and idly rowing
through clear waters through which
architectural masterpieces can be
glimpsed below (above right).

Flooded London was exhibited
at Medcalf Gallery as part of the
month-long London Festival of
Architecture in 2008.

D'espresso
Nemaworkshop

A library has been turned on its side to create the interior of this espresso bar on Madison Avenue in Manhattan. Books line the floor, pendant lights protrude horizontally from one wall and parquet flooring covers another, giving the impression that the whole room has been rotated through ninety degrees.

The coffee bar is located in close proximity to the New York Public Library in Bryant Park, which inspired the design. New York design studio Nemaworkshop took a life-size photograph of library shelves and printed it on tiles, which line the floor, ceiling and back wall.

D'espresso is a fledgling coffee shop chain and this, its second store, is intended to give the brand a strong image that will help it stand out as it grows.

Food Printer
Philips Design

Instead of preparing and cooking raw ingredients, consumers could one day press a series of buttons and stand back as a machine prints them a perfectly balanced dinner.

A food printer, such as this one proposed by Philips Design, would allow users to select the most appealing combination of flavours and nutrients, which could then be materialised as food in an unlimited range of spectacular forms.

Philips Design, the design department of Dutch electrical goods giant Philips, developed the food printer concept as part of Food Probe, a 2009 research project investigating how people will source and eat food 15-20 years from now.

The research focussed on three areas: food creation, whereby existing 3D printing technology could be adapted to the kitchen, which involved the printed food shown here; diagnostic kitchen, which explored devices that could scan the nutritional value of foods to help people consume a personalised healthy diet; and home farming, which investigated ways of allowing people to grow the food they need in domestic food factories.

The Food Probe project addresses serious issues, including the need to feed a growing global population from finite natural resources. It also tackles the challenge of shifting public opinion on scientific advances in food production, such as genetic manipulation, to become socially acceptable.

Wall House
FAR frohn&rojas
architects

A concrete box, greenhouse and tent all rolled into one, this low-budget retirement home in a field on the outskirts of Santiago de Chile abandons the traditional distinction between indoors and outdoors.

Instead of windows and walls, the building uses concentric layers of different materials that provide diminishing degrees of enclosure and protection from the elements.

These layers get lighter and more amorphous as you move from the solid core of the house to the exterior. The innermost layer is a two-storey, cast concrete shell that contains two bathrooms. This is the most private part of the house.

The second layer is a timber and plywood bookshelf. Open in some places and solid in others, this provides storage as well as enclosing the kitchen and other rooms.

The third layer is composed of high-insulation polycarbonate panels. Enveloping the structure like wrapping paper, this layer creates a double-height living space and the bedrooms.

The final layer is a fabric membrane that provides further solar shading, with voids that allow cool breezes to enter.

Published on Dezeen in 2007, Wall House was one of the first architectural projects to gain worldwide recognition through the internet rather than the traditional printed press. As a result, Chilean architects FAR frohn&rojas began selling sets of plans so people could build their own Wall House.

Champions
Konstantin Grcic

Sports equipment is covered in colourful graphics that suggest speed and performance, but contemporary furniture is usually devoid of such applied text or pattern. Industrial designer Konstantin Grcic questions this disparity by borrowing the graphic language of skis and racing cars, and unexpectedly applying it to a domestic object.

The Champions series, created in spring 2011 for an exhibition at Galerie kreo in Paris, is a set of eight different glass-topped tables with splayed aluminium legs. The rich graphics, painstakingly built up in layers of lacquer, are nonsensical, featuring made-up words. The idea however is to challenge designers' assumptions about the appropriate surface treatment for a product.

Gravity
Ziiiro

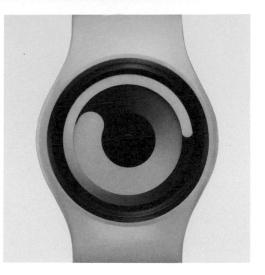

Gravity is a watch that discards as many of the conventions of traditional timepieces as it can, becoming a piece of abstract jewellery while retaining – just about – its timekeeping function.

Instead of hands, numbers and markings, it features two rotating discs, each printed with a coloured comet-like symbol that represents the hours and minutes. With the hours marked on the inner ring and the minutes on the outer one, the wearer tells the time by the position of the discs relative to the case.

Instead of a traditional strap, the product features a silicone rubber bangle stiffened by a strip of stainless steel. The watch slips over the wrist and is adjusted by squeezing together or pulling apart the bangle until it grips sufficiently to stay in place.

The strap can be removed, allowing it to be paired with a different-coloured watch face, or with another face from Ziiiro's growing collection.

Ziiiro is a designer watch brand based in Hong Kong. Gravity, its first product, was launched in January 2011 and was quickly followed by Aurora (which tells the time with translucent, overlapping coloured discs) and Orbit (which has planet-like dots instead of hands).

Urban Camping
import.export
Architecture

Urban Camping is a high-rise campsite that allows tourists to pitch their tents on elevated platforms erected in city centres.

The temporary vertical campsite, by Belgian architects import.export, has four stacked platforms connected by a ladder.

The 10-metre tall steel structure was first installed in Antwerp in April 2009 for an exhibition of mobile architecture at the Kaailand Festival. The platforms were fully booked by festival-goers. It was later installed in Copenhagen in 2009 and Antwerp in 2010.

The project was the result of a study into informal and spontaneous camping in urban areas and was developed in response to the demand for cheap short-break accommodation in cities.

The camping platforms are between 1.9 metres and 2.5 metres in diameter. Each platform has a green polyester net balustrade and is lined with a thin water-draining layer topped with artificial grass.

The architects also propose a permanent version that would become a vertical urban garden, with planted platforms and vegetation growing over the frame.

Open-air Library
KARO

This library never closes, doesn't employ any staff, and keeps all its books outdoors.

Built on the overgrown site of the old district library in Magdeburg in former East Germany, the Open-air Library operates entirely on trust, lending books donated by residents at any time of day or night.

The library doubles as a small public park, with bookshelves and reading areas set in niches within a wall running along one side of the plot. The aluminium façade of a 1960s modernist warehouse has been recycled to give the library an urban presence.

The library began life as a temporary intervention of stacked beer crates in 2005. The local community continued the momentum by setting up a library on the site. Open-air Library was later built as a permanent replacement, opening in June 2009.

The unconventional library was designed by German architects KARO and has won numerous awards, including the Architecture Award at the 2011 Brit Insurance Design Awards.

Havaianas
Isay Weinfeld
Arquiteto

In 2009, a store selling flip-flops
opened on one of the most
exclusive retail streets in São Paulo.

The Havaianas store on Rua
Oscar Freire was designed by
Brazilian architect Isay Weinfeld,
who played on the economic
disparity between the cheapness
of the product and the swankiness
of its location.

It is the cult Brazilian flip-flop
brand's first Brazil store and
Weinfeld wanted the exterior to fit
into the upmarket streetscape while
designing the interior to reflect the
origins of the products, which were
first sold at the city's street markets.

During opening hours the entire
shop front is open, free of doors
and window displays and marked
only by the Havaianas brand name,
formed of red 3D letters.

The entrance of the store is
designed to resemble a public square
with no products in sight. A broad
staircase descends to the shop itself,
which is a double-height space with
tropical planting along each wall.
Glass panels in the roof create an
informal, outdoor atmosphere.
Flip-flops hang in rainbow stripes
on the walls and a market stall
recalls the origins of the brand.

Havaianas created their first pair
of flip-flops in 1962. The now iconic
products were modelled on the Zori,
a traditional Japanese sandal, which
has fabric straps and rice straw
soles. One of the distinctive features
of Havaianas is the textured rice
pattern foot-bed that makes a visual
reference to this heritage.

Minimalist Effect in the Maximalist Market
Antrepo

Supermarket shelves would look very different if minimalist designers had their way: this project from 2010 suggests how some of the world's most famous brands could be simplified without losing their graphic identities.

Istanbul design consultancy Antrepo removed images and patterns from the labels of items such as Pringles, Nutella and Mr Muscle in stages, reducing the graphics to simple text and using no more than two colours.

The project explores whether global brands overload their products with unnecessary detail, and whether this approach is appropriate to information-age consumers. In Dezeen's comments section, readers tended to agree that the stripped-down packaging is more beautiful, but potentially confusing for shoppers.

Antrepo subsequently came up with a further refinement, called More Minimalist Effect in the Maximalist Market, removing everything from the packaging except key colours and text, which is all set in Helvetica Neu Bold. Devoid of logos, illustrations and bespoke fonts, products such as Guinness, Duracell batteries and M&Ms are still instantly recognisable.

National Stadium Beijing Herzog & de Meuron

Swiss architects collaborated with a Chinese artist to create the bird's nest-shaped stadium that is the most visible symbol yet of China's emergence as a superpower.

The National Stadium Beijing, built for the 2008 Olympic Games, was designed by architects Herzog & de Meuron with artist Ai Weiwei, who developed the concept for the woven pattern of steel beams that encloses the stadium bowl.

The bird's nest metaphor, which refers to an expensive Chinese delicacy, helped ensure the stadium's popularity.

The nest-like structure was originally conceived to support a retractable roof, which was an early requirement of the stadium's design. The roof was later dropped from the brief but the iconic lattice form was retained.

Herzog & de Meuron worked with structural engineers Arup to calculate the complex geometry of the steel, which is a mixture of structural components and purely aesthetic elements. Staircases located in the void between the lattice and the bowl follow the rake of the slanting beams (pictured).

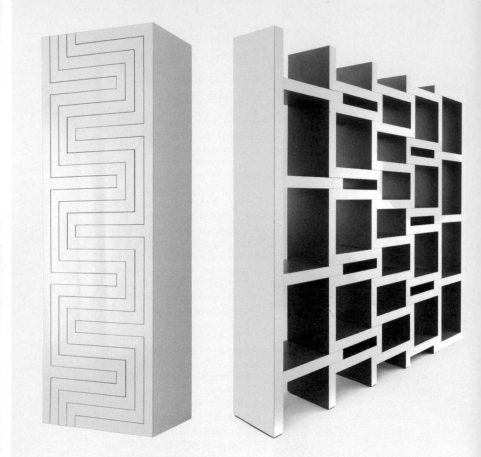

REK Bookcase
Reinier de Jong

REK is a bookcase that expands and contracts according to the size of your book collection.

It consists of five interlocking forms that can be pulled apart to create additional shelf space, or pushed together to save floor space. The two outer forms resemble more conventional shelving towers, while the inner three are zig-zag in form, designed to slot into each other. The bookcase appears full however much you have to display.

This simple product by Dutch designer Reinier de Jong was published on Dezeen in December 2008 and has proved to be one of our most enduringly popular stories. De Jong has since brought out the REK coffee table, which pulls out to create more surface area on top and storage underneath for magazines.

Land of Giants
Choi + Shine
Architects

Pylons in the form of giant human figures march across the landscape in this proposal by American architects Choi + Shine.

In 2008, Icelandic power company Landsnet held a design competition to find ways of minimising the environmental and visual impact of electricity transmission lines.

In Iceland, 80 per cent of power is derived from sustainable sources, such as hydropower and geothermal plants, but electricity has to be transmitted large distances across pristine landscapes.

With their Land of Giants submission, Choi + Shine turned conventional thinking about pylons on its head, proposing structures that would be more, not less, visible.

Based on a traditional steel pylon, the 45-metre figures are designed as a kit of parts that can be configured into different postures: crouching down as the lines cross hilltops; stretching up as they traverse valleys; the anthropomorphic pylons even bow their heads respectfully as they carry electrical burden past historic sites.

Choi + Shine didn't win the competition but received an honourable mention. The organisers subsequently put development of the winning project on hold, but Land of Giants has marched on, receiving widespread attention and provoking debate on whether large-scale infrastructural intrusions can enhance, as well as destroy, the landscape.

The Toaster Project
Thomas Thwaites

You can buy a toaster in a high street store for less than £5.00. Or you can attempt to make one yourself from scratch, extracting raw materials from the earth, processing them and turning them into components, then eventually assembling these into the final product.

Royal College of Art student Thomas Thwaites attempted the latter for his 2009 graduation show. The Toaster Project was an attempt to highlight the sophisticated global supply chains required to make even the most mundane product, but which often remain invisible to the consumer.

Thwaites did everything himself, from smelting iron ore that he collected in Wales in a homemade blast furnace to distilling crude plastic from oil. Instead of the 100-odd materials used in a basic toaster, Thwaites focussed on just five essential ones: iron for the grill, copper for the electrical plug and wires, plastic for the case and electrical insulation, nickel for the heating elements and mica for the heating element cores.

His quest to replicate a £3.99 Argos Value Range two-slice toaster took nine months and cost £1187.54.

132 5. Issey Miyake Issey Miyake's Reality Lab

Japanese fashion designer Issey Miyake has created a range of flat-pack shirts, skirts, trousers and dresses that resemble origami.

The angular garments, which were presented in Autumn 2010, are each made from recycled polyester that has been precisely folded to allow them to morph from flat geometric forms into wearable three-dimensional volumes.

The collection was inspired by the work of computer scientist Dr Jun Mitani, who uses mathematical methods to generate three-dimensional structures from folded paper. Called 132 5. Issey Miyake, the collection was created by research and development studio Reality Lab, which is run by Miyake with textile engineer Manabu

Kikuchi and pattern engineer
Sachiko Yamamoto.

A computer-modelling program
devised by Mitani was used to
design the clothes. Paper mock-ups
were then made to determine where
fold and cut lines were required to
flatten the forms.

There are ten basic flat patterns
available, from which many
garment designs can emerge by
varying the scale of the pattern and
combining different shapes.

Camper Stores
Various

While most fashion labels strive to unify their identity, quirky Spanish shoe company Camper has enlisted designers to create stores that are as diverse as possible.

In the last five years, Dezeen has reported on nine new Camper stores, all by upcoming designers, and each completely different. In a series of collaborations called Camper Together, designers have been allowed to express their own personalities in the interiors, rather than following corporate guidelines.

In 2011, Tomás Alonso's store in Covent Garden, London, opened. The interior is lined with ceramic tiles, which use geometric patterns to create optical illusions (above).

In 2009, Spanish designer Jaime Hayón referred to the circus when he designed the Tokyo store. The

door handles are in the shape of
candy canes and there are mirrors
on the ceiling, which distort
perspective (above right). Hayón
also designed Camper's store in Via
Montenapoleone in Milan, in 2007.

In the same year as Tokyo,
French designers Ronan and Erwan
Bouroullec created a store beside
the Centre Georges Pompidou that
features shoes displayed on fabric
panels in various colours that hang
on walls painted a deep red. »

» Again in 2009, for the brand's first Swedish store in Malmö, designers TAF were inspired by ice cream in their design for the interior. The colours used throughout the interior are based on ice cream flavours, including a vanilla-coloured concrete floor. The furniture is made of giant wooden ice lolly sticks (this page).

Camper has also commissioned store designs as part of the Camper Together initiative from Japanese designers Tokujin Yoshioka and Brazilian duo the Campana brothers, as well as a temporary display stand designed by Nendo.

Camper opened its first store in Barcelona in 1981 after several years of selling its shoes alongside other brands. It saw the opportunity to create interiors especially for enhancing the experience of the shoe consumer. The role of designers was crucial in developing the concept of self-service, where all styles are on display at once.

169

Merry-go-round Coat Rack Studio Wieki Somers

Visitors checking their coats in at the Boijmans van Beuningen art museum, Rotterdam, become part of an ever-changing performance artwork thanks to this cloakroom featuring a do-it-yourself system of coat hangers on pulleys.

The Merry-go-round Coat Rack occupies most of the entrance space. Red and white ropes, which are numbered, fan out across the ceiling via pulleys from a circular structure in the centre. The result is a form similar to a fairground carousel.

At the end of each rope is a rigid hanger-shaped loop on which visitors hang their coats, before winching them up towards the ceiling and securing them with lock and key. Jackets and scarves are then suspended in the air above head height.

Bags and other belongings are stored in racks of transparent, lockable boxes in and around the structure, where they resemble museum exhibits in glass cases.

Dutch designer Wieki Somers was inspired by stories of how Dutch miners used to securely store their belongings while working shifts below ground, tying them to ropes and winching them out of reach due to lack of storage space in the mine shaft.

Merry-go-round Coat Rack opened in 2008 and in the following year won the Golden Eye prize for best overall project at the Dutch Design Awards.

Hanger Chair
Philippe Malouin

Hanger Chair is a folding chair that doubles as a clothes hanger.

Looking for ways to save space in the home, Canadian designer Philippe Malouin noticed that folding chairs still take up valuable space between occasional use. So he set out to make them useful all the time.

Hanger Chair is made of three plywood components joined by a simple hinge mechanism. The hanger-shaped backrest has a hook at the top, allowing it to be hung from a clothes rail.

Malouin developed the Hanger Chair while studying at the Design Academy Eindhoven, where he exhibited it in 2008 as part of a series of space-saving objects. Other items included an inflatable dining table that packs away into a duffel bag when not in use.

Housing in Helsingborg Wilhelmson Arkitekter

The notion of the picture window has been taken literally in this design for a housing development in Sweden, which features irregular-sized windows surrounded by ornate gilded picture frames.

Envisaged by Swedish architects Wilhelmson Arkitekter in 2009, the development near Helsingborg would resemble an inside-out art gallery gazing across the sea to Denmark on the horizon.

The frames are designed to be made of cast aluminium covered in gold leaf, and are set in façades clad with white enameled panels.

The two stacked volumes contain 14 apartments that overlook the Øresund, a strait of water between Denmark and Sweden. It is at its narrowest point between Helsingborg on the Swedish coast and Helsingør, on the Danish island of Zealand, at two-and-a-half miles.

As inhabitants enjoy breathtaking views across the water, they would quite literally be on display to walkers on the seafront, giving new meaning to the term 'show home'. At the time of writing, construction of the housing had not yet begun.

As well as practicing as an architect, Anders Wilhelmson is a professor at the Royal Institute of Technology in Stockholm. Five months before the post on Helsingborg housing, Dezeen published another project by Wilhelmson at the other end of the spectrum – the Peepoo Bag (page 59).

Top ten #9

Playhouse Aboday

A house with a concrete slide instead of a staircase was the most popular story published on Dezeen during 2010 and one of the ten most popular of all time.

Playhouse by Indonesian architects Aboday features a spiral slide that links a child's bedroom to the kitchen. The slide is intended to provide the family's young son with a playful environment to counterbalance his strict education.

The house, near Jakarta, is one of several projects that features slides as integral parts of their design to have been featured on Dezeen. One, located in Tokyo and designed by Level Architects, has an enclosed slide linking all three floors, while an office in Tokyo by Schemata Architecture Office has a tubular slide accessed by a ladder.

Floating Observatories upgrade.studio and DSBA

Giant helium-filled balloons become panoramic elevators in this concept for a new type of skyscraper.

Eight leaf-shaped zeppelins capable of holding up to 80 people would move up and down tracks fixed to the façade of the tower. The floating observatories are different shapes and sizes, with the largest measuring 85 metres in length.

Proposed by Romanian architects upgrade.studio and DSBA with American designer Mihai Carciun for Taichung City, the idea won the Taiwan Tower Conceptual International Competition in 2010.

The design is based on a high-tech tree with the observatories acting as moving leaves.

Eiffel DNA
Serero
Architects

This competition-winning design to transform the Eiffel Tower – by adding a flower-like viewing platform at the top – turned out to be a fraud. The project appeared on the website of Serero Architects in March 2008; they claimed to have won a contest to temporarily make over the Parisian landmark to mark its 120th birthday.

Consequently Dezeen, along with several other publications including The Guardian newspaper in the UK, published seductive images of the iconic tower reimagined by the addition of a Kevlar structure that mimicked the lattice framework of Gustave Eiffel's 1889 structure.

Called Eiffel DNA, the fantasy project was designed using a generative computer script that identified the tower's genetic design code and used this template to 'grow' a structure, which would most efficiently support the temporary platform.

It wasn't until a few days later that the New York Times established that the competition was non-existent, and we admitted we'd been duped.

The episode was a sobering reminder of the ease with which false information can spread on the internet; it was also a brilliant PR exercise by the French practice, which received worldwide publicity. We still love the design, too.

Crumpled City
Emanuele
Pizzolorusso
for Palomar

These maps can be screwed up into a ball and stuffed away in a bag.

There are 17 Crumpled City maps, covering major cities like Berlin, London and Rome. Milan designer Emanuele Pizzolorusso

created the series for Italian brand Palomar to alleviate the frustrations of trying to fold a map along the original creases. Unlike paper maps, Crumpled City is resistant to damage from wind, rain and excessive folding. They are made of high-density polyethylene, which is strong, lightweight and waterproof.

Each map includes a list of 10 'SoulSights' – places brought to life by the people that inhabit them. They first went on sale in 2010.

House with Balls
Matharoo
Associates

Concrete balls on cables counterbalance rows of shutters that
regulate light and temperature in
this home in India.

House with Balls, set in farmland
outside Ahmedabad, has the dual
function of being a weekend retreat
and a place for the owner to breed

fish for his aquarium shop. The
design and choice of materials are
focussed on meeting a low construction budget. The house only cost
£7,500 to build and the handmade
concrete balls that animate the
simple exterior were specified as the
cheapest solution for the job.

Indian architects Matharoo
Associates designed the oblong
building, which consists of a
13-metre long living room enclosed
by metal shutters on both sides. The

shutters lift upwards to reveal a
garden on one side and four 9,000-
litre fish tanks on the other. The
balls are lowered to raise the
shutters and when fully open they
dip into the water on the tank side.

Although the house was built
in 2004, architectural photographer
Edmund Sumner visited India in
2010, supplying photographs for
Dezeen's story. The project was later
awarded the AR House 2010 Award
for the best house of the year.

OLA folding table
AKKA

While most folding tables need to be flipped upside down to be collapsed, OLA, by young Swedish studio AKKA, can be dismounted without any complicated manoeuvres.

The design comprises two legs that fold inwards and a leaf that drops down, meaning it can be put away in just three movements. The flipper-like legs give the lightweight table stability even when collapsed, allowing it to be self-supporting when stored without needing to lean against a wall.

OLA has a laminated plywood top and extruded die-cast aluminium legs, coated in white lacquer. The table is less prone to damage than conventional models since its surface is never laid on the ground and it is less likely to be chipped or scratched during manhandling. In addition, it requires only one person to set up or dismount.

AKKA was founded in Gothenburg by Petter Danielson and Oscar Ternbom. Named after Danielson's father, the OLA table earned the graduates joint-first place in the [D3] Contest for young designers at the imm cologne furniture fair in January 2011. Swedish manufacturers Materia have since put the table into production.

LunaTik
Scott Wilson

When Chicago designer Scott Wilson approached leading accessory brands with his idea for a kit that transforms Apple's iPod Nano into a multi-touch watch, they all turned him down. So instead he decided to manufacture it himself.

The outcome was a viral sensation that saw Wilson raise a million dollars in just one month and become the poster boy for a new generation of entrepreneurial designers who are finding new ways of getting their ideas to market.

Wilson's design, called LunaTik, consists of a high-grade aluminium case that holds the iPod Nano with a silicone rubber strap, allowing the user to access all the functions of the Nano – including the built-in watch – without removing it from their wrist. A second product called TikTok does the same thing but with a snap-in stainless steel housing and a lower price tag.

In November 2010, the designer put his idea up on Kickstarter – an online 'crowdfunding' platform that allows creative people to get their ideas funded by pre-selling products to customers. This system generates cash without the designer giving up control to equity-taking investors.

Wilson needed to raise around £9,000 to produce his product but within a month he had accumulated over £625,000. The story became an internet sensation and a few months later, the first editions of LunaTik and TikTok went on sale.

Unsustainable
Greetje
van Helmond

Crystals formed from everyday materials such as salt and water (in the form of ice) can appear every bit as beautiful as precious stones, but are not particularly prized for making jewellery.

This observation prompted Dutch designer Greetje van Helmond to produce a range of jewellery from sugar. The crystals that decorate the collection are grown in-situ by suspending unadorned necklaces and bracelets in a saturated sugar solution; sugar crystals begin to form naturally along the thread, growing larger over time. It can take a couple of weeks to grow the largest crystals, which are more robust than the extremely fragile ones that form in the first few days of the process.

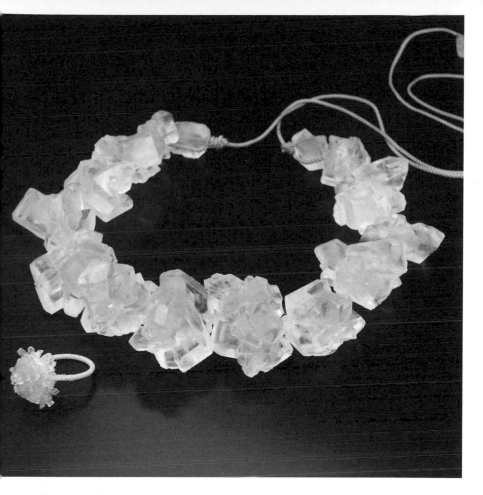

Van Helmond called her collection Unsustainable as both a comment on today's throwaway culture, and as an admission that jewellery made from sugar will not last particularly long if worn.

The collection was first shown in 2007 as part of van Helmond's graduation show at the Royal College of Art in London.

Recovery Lounge
Priestmangoode

The name alone suggests a radically different approach to hospital design. Rather than a ward, which conjures images of rows of beds, this is a lounge where people can relax. As opposed to focussing on the illness or the medical procedure, it is a place for recovery.

Recovery Lounge is a self-initiated project by Priestmangoode. The industrial designers have extensive experience in designing interiors for passenger jets, hotels and airports, and wanted to see if they could apply the lessons learned in those sectors to the neglected area of hospital interiors.

Intended for people recovering from minor operations, the lounge offers each patient their own zone, which is carefully oriented to maximise privacy. These zones are designed for comfort as well as efficiency, with furniture raised above the floor to allow easier cleaning, and push-button reclining beds like those found on aeroplanes.

The lounge borrows its staggered layout from first-class airline cabins, allowing more beds per square metre and improving sight lines, so staff can easily monitor patients and attend to their needs in a shorter amount of time. This in turn could save money by reducing the number of nurses required.

Recovery Lounge is part of a report published in 2010 by Priestmangoode called the Health Manifesto, which looks at how better hospital design could lead to health benefits for patients and significant cost savings for the NHS.

Moving Platforms
Priestmangoode

Long-distance journeys by rail could be faster if trains no longer stopped at stations along the way. That is the basis of the Moving Platforms proposal unveiled in spring 2011 by London-based design studio Priestmangoode.

Instead of making repeated stops, the high-speed trains would transfer passengers to a local service while still moving, slowing down to allow trams to draw up alongside and dock by aligning with its doors. People could then simply walk between the two vehicles.

Once the transfer is complete, the doors on both trains would close and the fast train would speed on to its destination, while the local train peels off and delivers passengers to their station.

High-speed trains are twenty-first century machines running on nineteenth-century infrastructure, but the cost of upgrading the network has prevented trains from competing against planes on long-distance routes. The act of slowing down and stopping at multiple stations, then accelerating away again is a legacy of the steam era. This dramatically increases journey time and decreases the efficiency of modern trains.

Priestmangoode believes that innovations such as Moving Platforms would help to make intercontinental train services a viable, and sustainable, alternative to air travel.

Sleepbox
Arch Group

As the name suggests, Sleepbox is simply a box to sleep in. Deployed in public buildings such as airports, train stations and shopping centres, they could be rented for periods ranging from 15 minutes to several hours, allowing people to take a nap without checking into a hotel.

The concept was unveiled by Russian architects Arch Group in 2009. The design is a utilitarian pod containing a bed, a TV, storage for luggage, power sockets for charging laptops and phones, and Wi-Fi. Bed linen changes automatically between guests, unwinding from a spool at the head of the bed onto another at the foot.

Capsule hotels offering compact, no-frills accommodation at airports or city centres have become popular in recent years, and Sleepbox is a logical development of the concept.

The air-conditioned capsules, which measure 2 metres by 1.4 metres and 2.3 metres in height are intended to be placed in clusters to form open-plan micro hotels, with customers using their credit card to check into a box.

The story garnered over 100 comments from readers when it was published on Dezeen in November 2009, with many expressing excitement at the prospect of having somewhere to lie down during long airport layovers. Some readers however expressed doubts over how the boxes would be cleaned, and were concerned that they would attract prostitutes.

The first Sleepbox has yet to open at the time of writing.

Humlegården apartment
Tham & Videgård

The owners of this large apartment in Stockholm wanted it refurbished in a style that moved away from the stereotypical Scandinavian blonde-wood look, so their architects instead gave them multi-coloured floors and walls.

The four-bedroom apartment, in a grand turn-of-the-century block next to Humlegården Park in the wealthy Östermalm district, had previously been used as a hotel and retained few of its original features.

Swedish architects Tham & Videgård proposed an interior scheme based on the seasonal colours of the neighbouring park, devising patterned floors of over-sized ash parquet that replicate the greens, yellows, reds and browns of the changing foliage.

The colours flow and merge throughout the apartment, linking rooms together in an ever-changing sequence. The 60 by 20 centimetre parquet panels have also been used on the walls in places, while doors and full-height shelving assume the same palette as the floor. »

» By adopting this multi-hued approach, the architects were conspicuously following in the footsteps of Swedish artists including Arts and Crafts painter Carl Larsson and architect and designer Josef Frank, rather than the more recent exponents of the pared-down Scandinavian modern look. Larsson (1853-1919) painted scenes of family life in traditional Swedish interiors while Frank (1885-1967) is famous for his vibrant textile designs.

To contrast with the floor and walls, the furniture and lighting selected for the apartment is all white (although the photographs shown here were taken before the apartment was furnished).

Tham & Videgård also designed The Mirrorcube tree house-style hotel room that features on page 100 of this book.

Stack
Shay Alkalay of
Raw-Edges

Israeli designer Shay Alkalay of
Raw-Edges Design Studio has
deconstructed the standard chest
of drawers and come up with a
version that can be opened from
both sides.

Conceived as a centrepiece
rather than something to be pushed
against a wall, Stack is a multi-
coloured storage system with no
visible frame or back. Instead,
drawers of varying depth are
stacked directly on top of one
another to create a sculptural tower.

In line with Alkalay's observation
that chests of drawers look more
intriguing when the drawers are
left partly open, Stack is designed to
look best when the drawers are
arranged irregularly, although they
can equally be made to align to
form a uniform pile.

Stack was put into production by
British manufacturers Established
& Sons and launched in April 2008.
It is made of birch plywood,
fibreboard and steel, and available
in versions with either eight or
thirteen drawers. The furniture
piece comes in shades of green or
red, as well as neutral wood veneer.

Stack won the Best Furniture
Design Award at the Homes &
Gardens Awards 2009.

Links
and credits

An online version of this section can be found at: dezeenbookofideas.com

201

The publisher would like to
thank all contributing designers,
architects, manufacturers,
institutions and photographers for
their kind permissions to reproduce
their images in this book.

Index

About Dezeen

Dezeen was launched by Marcus Fairs in November 2006 and grew rapidly to become the world's most influential design website. From the outset the site had a simple mission: to publish a carefully curated selection of the latest architecture, interiors and design projects every day, including work by both leading figures and upcoming talent.

Dezeen was one of the first design sites to adopt the now-ubiquitous blog format, which has changed the nature of publishing and allowed small companies, or even dedicated individuals, to reach audiences far greater than publications in print.

Sites like Dezeen have also changed the way that audiences react to architecture and design stories. Where once they had to write to magazines to get their views across, readers can now add comments to blog posts and interact via social media sites.

The original www.dezeen.com blog is now part of a growing family of sites, including recruitment website www.dezeenjobs.com, video site www.dezeenscreen.com and www.dezeenwatchstore.com, which sells selected watches by named designers and boutique brands.

The Dezeen sites collectively attract over one million visitors every month from around the world; this number is growing all the time.

Dezeen Book of Ideas is Dezeen's first paper-based publication, and is one of the first examples of a design website taking its content into print, rather than the other way round. The book has been designed by Micha Weidmann, who is responsible for Dezeen's website design.